AT HOME
FIGURES
edited by Rosa Branciaroli and Ilvi Capanna

Cover: Ettore Spalletti, Salle des Departs, Garches, 1996 - reducing graphical Patrizia Leonelli

Ettore Spalletti, Salle des Departs, Garches, 1996

Back home — introduction by Pepe Barbieri — 4

1. Small and simple — Ilvi Capanna — 8

2. Shapes & identity — Paola Branciaroli — 28

3. Inseparables — Massimiliano Scuderi — 44

4. The single-family house from the garden city to the urban sprawl — Carlo Pozzi — 56

5. Conurbations & detached houses — Rosa Branciaroli — 78

6. A piano for Fontanelle — Carlo Pozzi — 92

7. Compression & dispersion — Ilvi Capanna — 104

8. Appartences — Paola Branciaroli — 124

9. Two projects — Ivan Di Naccio, Marco Di Felice — 134

Back home

Pepe Barbieri

The two small side attached houses by Ettore Spalletti evoke a circular path in the cover of this book. They are part of his contribution to the *Salle des départs* of Garches hospital in 1996. They are houses, but at the same time tombs. As the impressive one of Cyrus of Persia, raised on a high pedestal. Immersed in the ever-changing liquid blue of the place of "departure", of the final greetings. The last resting-place, where one waits and stops. But it is constructed in an elementary way as the first type of shelter is: the hands gathered together as a roof over your head are evoked, as a protection.

So the first house - the first uncertainly designed during childhood - is linked to the last one.

One wonders how people are aware of the reference - also testified in this book - to the deepest meaning of these archetypes. Perhaps, the aspects more connected to a playful imagination prevail: in them the simple figure stands as an anchor for the memory, to find the pretext of a known and recognizable shape in a confused storage of images without quality.

Because today the stability evoked by the same terms - house, living - is threatened by a very different way of considering and using spaces. Regarding this, Gausa wrote on the number 20 of PPC about the emergence of a new consciousness of home life, "*...wandering and externalized, gradually spreading into the metropolis: the simultaneousness of private space with a service area spread at a urban level, in a city turned into a great "scattered house" for a nomadic user*". That prophecy (Argan, 1984) considered the city not as a defined area nor as an expanding space, but as an extended and continuous system of services with a virtually unlimited potential.

However, we must recognize the "high" and "heroic" appearance of this different dimension of living corresponds only partially to the ways in which a shower of houses is poured out on our territories changing the landscape and the working system. Rather, they are furiously introverted realities, almost indifferent to the relationship with the contexts. "*I am proud of my bathrooms and I do not want to know where they flush. The number of rooms is my domain. I block and I am blocked, I live between two amnesties and I do not care the external disaster*". F. Columbo.

It is, then, an overall transformation taking place without asking anything to the architecture, especially without concern for the "public meaning" of every single episode. Nowadays, the most dangerous comparison is between an individual conception considering the right to built a living space and a different idea, focused on the need to generate a

Pepe Barbieri

dialogue between individual freedom and a shared, public shape, recognizable in the commitment to draw a new landscape anyway. Rightly, the essays in this volume subtlety wonder about this crucial point. It is not a new question because the Modern research raises the question of how to combine the individual freedom of the traditional ways of house construction with the rules and opportunities of industrialization, of mass production. As Behne noted, all this lies within the civil task of *public responsibility* of the generated shape. Hence the many experiments on extension or modification, also with the strategic use of the free plan. For example, in 1931 and 1932 M. Wagner dealt with the extensible house with the "Sonne Luft und Haus für Alle" exhibition in Berlin.

It is a research related to the working system and the reconsideration of how the house is used. However, the concept of "good use" of the house expands, from one tied to the "internal" function of the house, a *private good*, to that of a *public good*, in which, according to the rationalist theorem, the function of housing and therefore its shape is determined in relationship with the new social and economic space as it is interpreted or desired. This is the premise of the Modern Movement research on the topic of housing. Considering the functionality of a machine, not only is accepted the accuracy of its operation, but also the accuracy of its production. The exact production of the house-machine is not far from the "precise for profession" production of the farmer's house *instrument* on his land. The here mentioned Renna's reflection on the continuity in Abruzzo, for example, of the experience of the dwelling construction returns, among the types of houses in the city and in the countryside. Even in the experiences of the Modern era in many cases it is possible to verify that there are different searches, according to a different idea of the city, to inherited housing types: the row house, side attached houses, court houses, tenements with communal balconies. In many cases, these types are reaffirmed in their original status, obscured and lost in the compact city of the nineteenth century.

The reflections and experiments presented in this book are included in this thematic horizon: how to avoid the production, through clusters of detached houses or trivial parcellings-out, of an inhabited one-dimensional and mono-functional territory, devoid of the most important quality the urban condition expresses with its complexity of uses and shapes. A research that can be linked to a new way of understanding the relationship between design and context: it is not an adaptation, but its construction. It is a question of *mobilitizing* the same context for the production of new *urban-territorial configurations*, according to a way for which the "rural" metaphor substitute, in the construction of the city, the "industrial" one: the urban countryside, the Agronica by Branzi, the Urbaparco by Toraldo di Francia. The quality of these new landscapes made of the "simple houses" cannot be entrusted only to the methods of building moulding - its is a practice little required and adopted - but also to the ability to give shape and role, in a creative interpretation of contexts, a different hierarchy of materials and signs: *the soil, roads, boundaries, common services, public spaces, new devices for energy production.*

After all, William Morris talks about an architecture that *represents all the changes and alterations made on the Earth's surface, according to human needs, except for the pure desert.*

Cyrus's tomb in Pasargadae

1

Small and simple

Ilvi Capanna

Cabane Vauban, baie du Mont-Saint-Michel

MVRDV, island Hagen to Ypenburg, 2001
Photo by Paola Branciaroli

10 Small & simple

In the last decades, the *elementary figure* of the house emerges in the architecture of research and stands out with some evidence. There are many experiences, even very different among each other, such as the residential unit designed by MVRDV studio for the island of Hagen in Ypenburg, the slit house in Nanjing by AZL Atelier, Walter house in Malans by Bearth and Deplazes, Rudin House by Herzog & de Meuron.

Here "...the element of inspiration is the house, the traditional house, the house par excellence, the archetype, the source and essence of the house itself. In its strict approach, the project evokes a primordial and concise image as it is shown, for example, in the drawings and memories of childhood..."[1]. Fascinating experiences appreciated for their sense of measure: they have re-measured the theme of the house within architecture and life, leaving aside in some ways that formal experimentalism, now secular, through which its simple shapes, seen as the result of a process of millenary improvement meant to accept life in a safe but freer and freer space, "were overwhelmed by new absurd, plastic or pictorial, functional or emotional, etc., meanings, until becoming what they are today, an excuse, a field where modern architecture shows its versatility and measures its ambitions *on a smaller scale*"[2]. *This is a house*, we can finally say it again in front of it, and yet the reflection, the appeal and the relief do not cancel a doubt, a question. What happened to Loos' *sayable* houses, to Mies' research? What happened to Wittgenstein's house, to all those issues internal to the advancement of modern thought and at least in part are still open, reaching us? Certainly the relationship seems easier thanks to Tessenow's experience, but there is still a feeling of great distance. The problem analyzes this reflection in order to clarify some terms, and I think it is useful to retrace the stages of the latest events and the experiences of the debate on the theme of single-family detached house, trying to identify those fundamental issues in the Modern era, now reaching us. Do they bring along still open issues in this matter? Or do they bring issues that these experiences have now closed? And to what extent?

This is a topic where two different ways of seeing the same object converge. The detached house in its clearest expression. The one we can see, or remember, in rural settlements or isolated in nature. The one we can consider as an alternative to the city, or rather an internal alternative in setting up a large part of contemporary urban sprawl. The one we can imagine even in a pre-historic condition, even before the city, or as if it were in her genes, in its very early stages of definition. And the detached house at the time in which it is widely used in the construction of the modern city can be seen today in the outcomes of planning or in the urban sprawl, characterized by direct building interventions. For example, in the most basic parcellings-out where the single-family house is detached compared to the plot (often a minimum one), and where the contrast between the origin of this type of house and the new state of urban compression is evident. Or in more complex plans experimenting aggregative minimum standards, such as semi-detached or four-family houses, and where the elementary type of the house intersects other very different types such as the patio or the row.

This is a particular theme in some ways. On the one hand, it brings along a kind of synthetic image of the house. Although identifiable in a number of building traditions, it is a *model* which seems to lie beyond these traditions, beyond stylistic conditions or specific cultural areas, a model related to characteristics of the human condition independent from history, unchanged and constant over time. On the other hand, it is an issue of architecture as another, or rather we can see it as the theme of themes, the primary theme. Considered as such, it directly experiences, without mediations, the actual architectural working conditions, the difficult condition of architectural representation and of its figurativeness. I believe those simple houses pose a question: can very different, if not antithetical, working directions converge? On the one hand, we have paths more related to the human meanings and figurativeness of architecture; on the other hand, there are directions maintained within the limits of its practical experience, of its profession and within the conditions of its practice.

This problem certainly touches an aspect of the project that addresses the coexistence of experiences over time, one of the central issues in the complex process of critical review of the Modern era, started around the middle of the last century. It found a declaration point in the new Casabella, the *Casabella-Continuity* by Rogers, director from 1983 to 1963. The term *continuity* indicated one of the central aspects of that review, as opposed to the perhaps more reductive slogan of militant critics, namely the claimed break of modern architecture with the past.[3] It was the well known detailed investigation on the conditions of the problem of transmitting the past experience into the present in the Modern era, especially through the reading of the modern work of some of its masters[4]. Not only was that problem reduced to the educational aspect of transmitting experiences over time, but it also touched the quality of shapes of architecture, their potential figurativeness and their *needs*. The shapes cannot abandon the relationship with the past.

Instead, they need a sort of an inside ancient patina at the expense of their reason for existence, that is, survival, *La vie des formes*[5]. Traditions were always the great mediators between, on the one hand, the vastness and inconsistency of the past and its many stories, and on the other hand, the experience and the practice of shapes in the present[6]. In the Modern era, and even before, they suffered, together with the idea of *place*, from a slow and inexorable corrosion, even at the hands of their own defenders as the German Werkbund and the Viennese Werkstatte, up to the establishment of the *Kultur/Zivilisation* dichotomy[7]. Traditions gave finite shape to the *non-finite* past by ensuring the transfer *from hand to hand* to the present. Their impracticality in the transmission of experience maintains history as the only mediator with the past, and it is now a modern history, based on the critical method[8], which extends even more the vastness and inconsistency of time marked by humanity. "So, as it happens for the architectural culture, the history, the knowledge of the past through a *careful critical study of the recognized masterpieces* are understood as a tool meant to restore an endangered but not lost continuity. The relationship that should tie the present to the collective memory, sedimented in the tradition, would be then restored through a new role assigned to the historical knowledge. But this reference to history as a critical consciousness of the past can lead to anything but the renewed memories of that *interrupted melody*.... the sweet echo of the past resonating in the memory like a half-remembered music [Blomfield, Modernismus, London 1934]...."[9].

In 1943, Henri Focillon outlined in a few pages this new and in some ways terrible historical overview of *the life of shapes* from which some positive elements emerge, such as the possibility of establishing "spiritual families.... beyond time, beyond places"[10]. But the difficulty of the continuity of *the life of shapes* in the present emerges as well, a condition that is going to be purely historical[11]. Some masters of the Modern era had clearly experienced this difficulty and had placed it at the centre of their work. For example, Tessenow highlighted it when describing the sense of the flat roof for the Modern Movement. "... when we intentionally create a volume where the roof remains invisible, we act as the composer who voluntarily gives up to use certain notes. Such giving up may represent the ultimate mastery of the subject", and later on, when recognizing the flat roof as a new technical possibility of architecture like the others, he stressed "the fact that we are fighting in favour of a flat roof, we seek to improve it and in some cases we choose it - so to speak - because of its characteristic of denial...."[12], overcoming one of the typical forced choices of the Modern era, *assertion/denial*, through the concept of omission[13]. Of course, this issue affects architecture as a whole, but in the single-family house it gains even more evidence for several reasons.

First and foremost, regarding this issue, according to the architects of the Modern era some traditions were still close in some ways, still in progress at least in certain areas, even after the First World War, and not yet tainted by the abuses of the nineteenth-century formalisms. We have recently seen an example of it in the great movie by Michael Haneke, *The White Ribbon*, set in a small town in northern Germany in the early twentieth century, participating in that building tradition with which Tessenow will maintain, in its modern research, a peculiar relationship[14].

Secondly, the relationship with tradition seemed more necessary than for other topics, such as the collective residence or the public building, because that topic was more related to the individual family life, and therefore often resistant to issues regarding the new *style*. Then, it was also strictly related to the familiarity and recognition of architectural shapes. In *Il progetto di una piccola casa (The design of a small house)*, Giorgio Grassi clarifies this relationship through two necessary conditions: "The very idea of the house, its most immediate and genuine image,...the one that crosses uninterrupted the history of the man house... And then the specific quality of the house itself over time, namely, the constant prevalence of the *object of use* on the shape". Then he specifies the concept of space shaped by use "in the sense that such a space does not come into contradiction with the goal for which it is intended, where the different functions are considered with a sort of judicious foresight, so that the shape, although understanding the different functional elements, is never specifically determined"[15]. Carlo Manzo clarifies the concept of *object of use* through an excerpt from *Eupalinos*: "... Phaedrus: there are some wonderful tools, polished as bones. Socrates: they are almost self-made, at least to a certain point. Centuries of use have necessarily discovered the best shape. An incomparable experience reaches the ideal and settles down. The best efforts of thousands of people slowly converge towards the cheapest and most reliable shapes..."[16]. Each project is therefore a further act of improvement, the use value of architecture can exist precisely and only in relation to the experience of the past.

Finally, the ability to read the formal constant elements in very distant traditions due to the geographical location and period. For example, the persistence of the idea of the *house as a single room* described by Antonio Monestiroli as one of the central elements in the topic of the house especially in relation to the external complexity, "... where

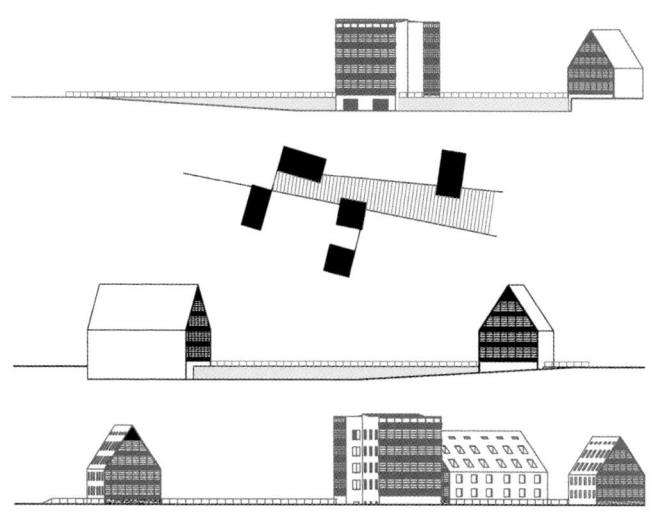

Project houses scattered, ideas competition for new urban residential projects in the urban periphery of Bergamo." project group: I. Capanna, R. Branciaroli, M. Scuderi, D. Lobefaro, L. Falconi, G. Barbieri, adviser

Frame from the movie White Ribbon by Michael Haneke

Ogimachi, Kanda house

16 Small & simple

it does not matter so much the internal layout of the house, but the place of overlooking, the place where this only large room is situated and the relationship it establishes with the city and the landscape"[17]. It also involves the internal spatial quality of the house, although we must distinguish between the archaic sense of an internal spatial unit, the cave, and the spatial unit of the house in its historical evolution, resulting in different basic types - the court, the tower, the row, the block - and crossing the functional modern specializations. However, it is always possible to find the leitmotiv of an experience always seeking the lost archaic unit and its freedom of use in a particular element - a large room or a porch - or in a particular definition of the distribution system. Modern research on this topic is often seen as rationalization of paths, search for the minimum space, etc. I believe instead that their contribution, such as those by Alexander Klein[18], lies in identifying the distribution system as the central architectural element of the modern house, that is to say, the need to investigate the shape, the spatial articulation. This complex system crosses and innervates all the individual spaces of the house, composed of heterogeneous elements - from the front door to the ladder, the higher spaces and the facings, closing the circle with an outward movement, like a window or a small balcony - a system that sometimes seems to stop while merging with parts of other spaces, such as the living room or the kitchen. Here the spatial articulation exists through the juxtaposition at a distance. Juxtaposition and perimeter, linearity and centrality, both pairs contribute to the complexity and identity of the distribution, seen as a spatial unit of the whole house.

Connected to this unit of the house, the persistence of a real shape can be found in the hut. This figure runs through the history of living in many and varied geographical areas and it is still very present in the architecture without architects, in the traditions closer to the origin as the most evolved ones, and even in prefabricated buildings.

Even in the essays on architecture between the eighteenth and nineteenth century, it stands out to mark a sort of watershed between the hypothetical reconstructions of the primitive house very close to nature, usually shaped with one material and one gesture, and those where the relationship with nature becomes - so to speak - more equal. It means that a set of shapes emerges, coming individually from nature, but they together lead to an aggregative code, a language different from the natural matrix of reference, the code that will also support the separation of the single element. Since the '50s of the last century the hut, and in general the archetypes of the house, reappears at the centre of numerous historical and philosophical studies, particularly those by

Gaston Bachelard and Mircea Eliade[19], to fit also into the thematic field of architecture with the book by Joseph Rykwert *On Adam's House in Paradise: The Idea of the Primitive Hut in Architectural History* published in 1972. Rykwert noted that the search of the hut is not a search for what was lost, but what cannot be lost. The hut is not the memory of an object, but a state of mind or consciousness, "... of something that existed, something that was done: an action. It is a collective memory kept alive within certain groups by means of legends and rituals, but it also seems to have occurred in circumstances in which, to explain its transmission and its survival, one cannot invoke the normal historical tradition. It would seem that it has an intrinsic connection to the idea that the man himself has of the products of its own activities and in particular to his conception of his shelters". This idea does not belong only to the distant past, but also to possible future perspectives. At the end, the book shows this relationship with the projective dimension: "... the interest in the primitive hut... seems alive with all peoples and at all times, and the meaning attributed to this processed image does not appear to have undergone many changes going from one place to another, from one epoch to another. I would also suggest that this meaning will persist in the future and will continue to have inevitable and constant consequences on the relationships between any kind of construction and its users... for all those who have something to do with the building, it will continue to be a model image of a primitive hut perhaps always placed beyond the kingdom of historians and archaeologists, in a place that I am forced to call paradise. And paradise is both remembrance and promise"[20]. We could read these archetypes in Tessenow's work, but here precisely the opposite happens. He works on a specific historical experience of architecture, a tradition, abandoning its inevitable synthetic aspect, not following it, that is so say, considering the consequences, but treating it the other way round. The goal is not to replace the original hypothetical archetypes, but to highlight the analytical aspect of that tradition, to take to pieces what had been composed in it. Thanks to this division the thread with past experiences can be tied again without traditions, even in an historical era. This breakdown cannot exceed certain limits: "whenever we strive to reach purity of shapes, there is the risk of falling into poverty instead, or even in the absence of formal language"[21]. Tessenow here referred to the need of a historically determined language against the universalist aspirations of neoplasticism. But his houses are far even from those of the traditionalists of his days. They are closer to Loos' houses. "For Loos, like all the *other great Viennese theorists of language*, ornament is every word that goes beyond its conditions of meaning, the formal rules of its grammar and syntax, the limits of its function. (For Schonberg, ornament is each repetition and each item not included in the fundamental compositive idea)"[22]. For Tessenow the smile of a poppy is included in the field of wheat, the whistling in the work of the craftsman.

The need to identify the limits of one's own work, the renunciation to the idea of the whole for the idea of the part corresponds to the loss of traditions. In the era of modern history the architect shuns the free shapes and, as a bricklayer persists considering them *necessary*, feels the duty to identify a research area, bounded by precise and mandatory limits. It is a partial perspective but because of this it is able to tie again the broken threads of its own language even through the twists and turns of a history increasingly devoid of old syntheses. In this sense, even very different experiences such as those of Tessenow, Loos, Mies, Hilberseimer show their closeness, their commonality of purpose: not to seek a new style, but to continue to work in a styleless time.

If one wants to find the necessary shapes in the absence of models, he/she cannot start from the shape, from a pre-established shape, but from a problem defined in a certain place and by a profession. As Mies said, what is worth is the process and the form is just a result.

Giorgio Grassi has certainly been the protagonist in the process of critical review and clarification of this Modern issue and of the rigour it has been analyzed with by some of his teachers, but he has also demonstrated its relevance, its inevitability even in contemporary architectural practice.

It is a big problem especially in case of a project for a small simple house. We would like this task to be devoid of complications and anxieties of research and instead "...it seems to have become, for a variety of reasons, a fairly complicated issue." Grassi identifies in the "absurd departure from the initial model" the underlying reason for this crisis, at least as regards the disciplinary responsibility, but distinguishes the image of the house, an essential component of that model, from any preconceived form. Its required shape can only be reconstructed analytically, as the result, not the premise. The image of the house is traced back to its more complex and general features that always distinguished the relationship, the expectation, between dweller and dwelling, "general notions such as solidity and durability, but also formal completeness, clarity and constructive logic." So the architect works on the thin thread that separates the sayable from the not sayable. The figurativeness of architecture is entrusted only to the right practice of the profession, "following the unbroken thread that links the house to daily life"[23]. This is a rigorous position whose design results demonstrate with increasing evidence a substantial advance in the architectural research, hardly circumscribed only in the field of personal poetics. This rigour seems to exclude the use of the hut, a possibility of procedure as elaboration of the model of the hut. But this figure has crossed the times and the world in the history of the house, even in very different cultures and traditions, and still continues to have great presence in the global settling scenery, where it is often free from the usual trappings and formalistic abuses.

We find it now, as I said, also in the architecture of research, in the work of even very different architects. This attests the need for a new figurativeness in architecture[24], for overcoming those limits the Modern era brought to light. To what extent do these limits still belong to our time? To what extent is their overcoming arbitrary? And can this overcoming be possible through a new comparison with building traditions? Is it still possible such a comparison? A comparison - so to speak - in the style of Tessenow?

In an interview, Jacques Herzog clearly states that the work of H&deM studio does not rely on any tradition, especially in Switzerland, but it reflects the idea of tradition, it raises the problem.[25] Can we have a figurativeness of architecture unfounded in a specific tradition, in a defined conventional system?

As a matter of fact, these experiences cannot be included in any specific building tradition. They rather seem to be placed *before* them trying to grasp the essential element, the common synthetic aspect from which the different traditions have spread, diversifying their codes. For example, one of their common features, that is, the tendency towards a material unity between layers of the roof and walls of the house, an effective unity achieved through a sophisticated technology, or alluded to through the choice of materials and colours, relocates the house in an archaic condition, before the process of individuation and specialization of its components. It seems this figure of the house embodies both primary archetypes of the house, the cave and hut. It funds the experience of the cave, of its material unit - the volumetric and material unit present in that archaic sense of the shelter considering this as a single space, simple and controllable, as opposed to the complexity and external infinity - with the representation of that materiality in the hut by means of the construction, in so far as the two archetypes seem to stand as the front-back of a unique pre-existing form of our collective unconscious. All this makes it possible in our time a strong figurativeness, a possibility of existence of the simple and practical in the total chaos of virtual-commercial formalism. But what constitutes

Cavern

Ypenburg house, MVRDV studio, 2001
Photo by Paola Branciaroli

Cape Cod House with Pediment
Photo © Jackie Craven

MVRDV, residential units Hageneiland

22 Small & simple

the strength also marks its limits. The aspect of familiarity, everyday life, normality that distinguishes the relationship with the house, what you want from it, throughout its history, is missing.

Obviously, individual experiences are very different among each other. A strong element of distinction can be identified in the sense the archetype takes and thus the figurativeness of architecture. In the most interesting experiences, I think the use of the archetype and the search for a new figurativeness of architecture is tied to more concrete, more specific aspects, elements of a profession that can operate independently from different models and figures.

In the residential unit designed by MVRDV studio for the island of Hagen in Ypenburg, the figure of the hut seems to take a typological sense, as the chess pieces on the chessboard, participating in a game and in its conventional rules, in the construction of a piece of city. The process of the project clearly emerges from the zenith sight. The installation of the four parts that make up the residential unit shows a kind of correspondence among the different isolated blocks, which seems to allude to the initial moment of the design process, where each of the four parts would be resolved with a single continuous line of row houses with the ridge parallel to the road. The second act of this hypothetical procedure sections the continuity of the row and shifts the obtained different-sized single blocks.

In this way the morphology of the unit is specified in relation to the presence of two very different elementary types, the side attached block and the detached block. However, this relationship keeps evident the two opposing principles we can even read in individual buildings, in the frequent blind walls or in the distributive solutions. In this way the figure of the hut tends to lose its status as a model to assume the status of result of the design project.

As far as the house in its architectural individuality is concerted, I think the *hut* by Herzog & de Meuron, Rudin house, goes beyond the simple recovery and processing of the archetype. Here, as in many other of their works, the figurative search includes again within the intellectual (and building) processes the dimensions always expressed by figures. "... We want to make sensual architecture which can't be experienced by the intellect alone, but which has a more immediate, more physical effect... even elements of smell"[26]. This new figurativeness of architecture is not defined in old or new areas, places and traditions, and seeks to go beyond the dichotomy figurativeness/abstraction, positively establishing itself within "... a possible compatibility between two poles in constant tension with each other: the fundamental identity- belonging principle and the non-place principle"[27]. The sensuality of the figure weaves relationships with a system of abstract remarks - proportions, types, conventions, etc. -. But these relationships cross a sort of sliding and difference space between the two systems, thanks to which the building communicates through the tension between figure and image.[28]

NOTES

1. This is what Ugo Baldassarri says referring to Rudin House, Area n°51 July/August 2000, Federico Motta Editore. I remember an experience, the *Case sparse (Scattered cities)* project, an ideas competition for the realization of new residential interventions in the Bergamo urban corona. Project team: I. Capanna, R. Branciaroli, M. Scuderi, D. Lobefaro, L. Falconi, consultant G. Barbieri. In: catalogue of Bergamo Alta exhibition, Social Theatre, July 1997.

2. G. Grassi, *L'architettura come mestiere e altri scritti*, FrancoAngeli, 1980

3. We find a summary of the debate, developed in those years, of the different protagonists and key issues in *Avanguardia e nuova architettura* by M. Scolari, in: AA VV *Architettura razionale* Milano 1979, collection of materials relating to the *International Architecture Exhibition of the XV Triennial* of 1973.

4. For example: H. Tessenow, *Osservazioni elementari sul costruire*, edited by G. Grassi Milano 1979, L. Hilberseimer *Mies van der Rohe*, edited by A. Monestiroli Milan 1984, *Adolph Loos Parole nel vuoto*, foreword by Joseph Rykwert, Adelphi 1992.

5. ...quelle est la place de la forme dans le temps, et comment s'y comporte-t-elle? Dans quelle mesure est-elle temps et en quelle mesure ne l'est-elle pas? D'une part l'oeuvre d'art est intemporelle, son activité, son débat propre s'exerce avant tout dans l'espace. Et d'autre part elle se place avant et aprés d'autre oeuvre. Sa formation n'est pas instantanée, elle résulte d'une série d'expériences. Parler de la *vie des formes*, c'est évoquer nécessaireiment l'idée de la succession.... H. Focillon *Vie des formes* Paris 1943

6. "... the term "tradition" essentially refers to what allows the transmission of values, ideas, behaviours through the continuous and live flow of a homogeneous community, rooted in a territory belonging to it.... In the contemporary world - where everything is formalized and rationalized, from manufacturing processes to personal and social relationships - that knowledge transferred from hand to hand, characterizing the community of the traditional world, will tend to extinguish....... This progressive abandonment of culture linked to tradition and experience dragged on throughout the past two centuries. However, it experienced a sudden and dramatic speeding up with the 1914-1918 war." G. Pigafetta, I. Abbondandolo, M. Trisciuoglio *Architettura tradizionalista* Milano 2002

7. F. Amendolagine, M. Cacciari *Oikos da Loos a Wittgenstein* Officina edizioni 1975

8. ".. The period when the critical method was set for the first time corresponds, in my opinion, to the period of setting the problem of the meaning of the work and its relationship with history, the new way to study it and the new way of understanding it as an experience."
G. Grassi *La costruzione logica della architettura* Marsilio 1967

9. G. Pigafetta, I. Abbondandolo, M. Trisciuoglio op. cit. "... Nothing is more distant from the history of collective memory. The story emerging from the critical digging into the past results from the different points of view from which the question on the same past is projected. The historical culture of modernity has rather shown this. It doesn't exist a history to anchor the present to, but the present itself produces multiple images of the past..... To rely on history in order to reconstruct a collective consciousness means to expose that consciousness to the very multiplicity of viewpoints, methods and historiographic tools. On the other hand, as Hans Georg Gadamer recalls, it is from the constitution of the modern idea of history that the link with tradition is irretrievably broken, opening up to modernity."

10. H. Focillon *Vie des formes* Paris 1943. The development of the type notion in architecture, so close to the concept of spiritual family, can be seen as the development of a necessary tool for the practice of forms in the Modern era conditions.

11. F. Ferrarotti *Il silenzio della parola* Daedalus 2003 "...If the past does not preserve itself in the tradition, it shifts to history books and museums.... In this sense Halbsachs believes that memory differs from history..."

12. H. Tessenow Il tetto in: Das neue Frankfurt 1926-1931 by G. Fats Daedalus 1975

13. G. Grassi, *L'architettura come mestiere, introduzione a H. Tessenow*; in: Heinrich Tessenow *Osservazioni elementari sul costruire* edited by G Grassi F. Angeli 1974

14. "... Tessenow often seems to explore in its projects the German residential tradition of those years [the early nineteenth century]. Tessenow seems to continue in that work of merging into a unique formal perspective local tradition and European architectural experience, whose results are so amazing in terms of their own strict authenticity...." G. Grassi *L'architettura come mestiere (introduzione a Tessenow)* 1974 ; in: *L'architettura come mestiere e altri scritti* FrancoAngeli 1980

15. G. Grassi *Il progetto di una piccola casa* in: *L'architettura come mestiere e altri scritti* FrancoAngeli 1980.

16. Paul Valéry Eupalinos ou l'architecte 1923, in: C. A. Manzo *Questioni di uso e forma in architettura* CLEAN 1984

17. A. Monestiroli La qualità del progetto di architettura: il progetto della casa.
in: L. Semerani (cura di) *La casa. Forme e ragioni dell'abitare* Milano 2008.
or Aldo Rossi: "... Distributive indifference is peculiar to architecture; the transformation of the old buildings... proves the

facts. It has the value of a law; the examples of the transformations of amphitheatres (Arles, Colosseum, Lucca, etc.) even before urban transformations mean that the highest architectural specification - in this case, a monument - potentially offers a greatest distributive potential, or more generally, the highest functional freedom." A. Rossi *Due progetti* in Lotus n.7 Venezia 1970

18. M. Baffa Rivolta, A. Rossari *Alexander Klein: lo studio delle piante e la progettazione degli spazi negli alloggi minimi: scritti e progetti dal 1906 al 1957* G. Mazzotta, 1975

19. In the first update to the volume of Carbonara, *Architettura pratica*, Giuseppe Strappa tells the story of project experiences and the debate on the dwelling house which, from the middle of the last century, "cast the seeds of doubt in the crystal certainties of modern architecture".
G. Strappa *La casa di abitazione* in: P. Carbonara Architettura pratica aggiornamenti vol. primo UTET 1989
Here it is noted the importance of studies like those of Gaston Bachelard *La poétique de l'espace* Paris 1957 and Mircea Eliade, Le sacré et le profane Paris1967 (written in the mid-'50s), and their influence on the architecture in the work of Joseph Rykwert *On adam's house in paradise: the Idea of the Primitive Hut in Architectural History* 1972 and Franco Purini La Casa 1979.
Within his phenomenology of the *imagination*, Bachelard introduces and develops the sense [of space] through the innate idea of the detached house, the archetype of the shelter. "The house, in the man's life, transcends the contingencies, multiplies its suggestions of continuity: if it missed, a man would be lost. It sustains the man through the storms of heaven and the storms of life, it is body and soul, it is the first world of the human being. Before being «thrown into the world», as metaphysicians declare, the man is placed in the cradle of the house and, in our *rêveries*, the house is always a big cradle." G. Bachelard *La poétique de l'espace* Paris 1957, tr. It. Dedalo 1975

20. J. Rykwert *La casa di adamo in paradiso* tr. it Mondadori 1977
21. op. cit. note 25
22. F. Amendolagine, M. Cacciari *OIKOS da Loos a Wittgenstein* Officina edizioni 1975
23. op. cit. note 2
24. Yvonne Volkart *Giving a glow to a given trace* Flash Art
In this interview, Herzog & de Meuron mention the discourse on the figurative and sensorial possibilities of contemporary architecture: "...*an architecture which can't be experienced by the intellect alone, but which has a more immediate, more physical effect. It shouldn't just have visual dimensions, but tactile or spatial ones too, even elements of smell."*

25. "......*Do you consider your work to be Swiss?*
Many people still imagine Switzerland as a small, isolated, traditional country and perceive our work as coming out of the tradition of the Swiss artisan. Nothing could be further from the truth. Switzerland has lost all these roots. Switzerland is perhaps the most modern, the most technologically advanced country in Europe. Of course it is also a very ambiguous country because it still keeps turning an attitude of peacefulness towards the outside, even if it deals with money and the big industry. This is a conflict which actually dominates more and more the political debates of this country: the awareness of being part of a global culture without any historical privileges left! If our work is in any way Swiss, it is so only in that sense of a country which has no national identity anymore. Our work is not based on any tradition, particularly any Swiss tradition. But it reflects the idea of tradition. It raises the question of tradition."
Jeffrey Kipnis *"A conversation with Jacques Herzog (H&deM)"* El Croquis n°84 1997

26. op. cit. note 11

27. G. Marramao *Appartenenza e atopicità*, in: Piano Progetto Città n° 14 Dipartimento di Architettura e Urbanistica, Università di Chieti 1994

28. I believe it is necessary to specify what I mean with image and figure in the representational play, in particular their differences. While the image breaks away from its object to build an autonomous entity, the figure always maintains a relationship with it because here the representation is partial, it only refers to one aspect, for example its silouette or its shadow, then it is also study, analysis of the object. While the image can exist thanks to its conciseness even without an existing object, the figure cannot simulate a non-existing object and it is comprehensible only within a conventional, almost defined, scenery.

2

Shapes & identities

Rosa Branciaroli

Aldo Rossi, House in Goito, 1979
From Aldo Rossi, Architetture 1959 - '87, Electa 1987

The residence is a fundamental criterion for the study of urban morphological issues and is a leading part in the construction of the city. The choices relating to the diverse and multiple residential areas peculiar to the contemporary condition cannot but be included in the overall system of urban relationships[1].However, especially in the "sprawling" suburbs of the contemporary city, it is problematic in general to find significant systems of relationship and belonging to the city as a whole. This is most evident if one refers to private building, in particular to the extensive construction of detached houses built in recent decades, scattered and fragmented on large areas, mainly related to pre-existing road layouts and incisively and simultaneously interested by systems of infrastructures and territorial, suburban services[2].

The alternative to the status of general morphological non-definition, contextual indifference and standardized banality of this type of residence is represented by design strategies that confer formal recognition and sense of belonging to it. The detached house represented and represents sill now a field of continuous experimentation of the architectural design, or rather the privileged object, certainly also for its limited dimensions, of a freer and often arbitrary formal interpretation. "In the collective imagination the detached house, more than a flat, holds together the archetypal elements of living: the embankment of the building, the roof, the fireplace, the fence. One tends to establish a relationship of identification with it, colonizing the interior spaces and defining his/her own territory to act freely"[3]. The theme of the detached house must be analyzed particularly in terms of historical and constructive continuity to understand and interpret with greater awareness its role and the possibilities of its formulation in the contemporary world. The project of the detached house is in this way a part of the path of historical knowledge of the subject and of the multiplicity of contextual relationships and significant references to the construction methods of contemporary architecture.

In the Modern era, the detached house building type, apart from the American experience, does not belong to the city, but is peculiar to the countryside and expresses its most evolved character with the *villa*. The introduction of the single-family detached house among urban houses is historically typical of the genre of experiences alternative to the high-density city. Claude Nicolas Ledoux is one of its most bright theoretician[4]. Ledoux participated in the big project of transformation of the city proposing its dispersion in the countryside. Ledoux defines the single-family detached house as it is, in *its own features* in direct contact with nature. The realization of the general idea of the city, the city surrounded by nature, goes through the design of individual buildings, "each according to its own features, manifested in nature distinguishing from it and at the same time nominating it as the only possible environment to be faced with"[5]. The XVIII century sets the necessary conditions for the development of the new type of building of the single-family detached house and its groupings. In the following century the research intensively continues through a variety of theoretical and planning concepts all meant to foreshadow new models designed to overcome the boundaries and conflicts of high-density urban settlements, regaining at the same time the relationship with nature. Owen, Fourier, Considerant and Cabet will design low-density residential blocks isolated in the countryside, related among each other, with manufacturing plants and public buildings "in order to rebuild the great new modern city integrated with the countryside according to totally new shapes and dimensions"[6]. Later, through a rationalization and renewal process, Ebenezer Howard's "garden city" will merge the instances of the expanding capitalist city and the nostalgia "for the medieval community "on a human scale"" [7].

The single-family detached house, within these and other similar models of that time, acquires a defined role and is part of a significant system of links and relationships, between building and plot, plot and isolated block, residential and public areas[8]. The huge number of studies and research later carried out by the Modern movement decisively identifies in its first stage, especially through the work of special interprets, the formal elements, the criteria for a housing architecture with a strong identity. The detached house described in these studies, as well as in the case of other housing types, is reinterpreted and redefined specifying issues of distribution, grouping and contextual relationship, including the dimensional and architectural clarification of formal elements. The systematic investigation on the minimum elements of the house in Alexander Klein is not separated from the attention to the intrinsic and identity values of the building and from new configurative hypotheses on plots and isolated blocks. In the project by Tony Garnier for an industrial city, an entire urban area is designed with single- or two-family detached houses, with all the possible variants of internal distribution. The entire system of buildings, plots, attached lands and public spaces, constitutes as a whole the residential area conceived as a constituent and integrated part of the general idea of the city. The search for an objective scientific methodology aims at the resolution of the specific problem of the house resulting from the demographic expansion of the most important urban centres. That search does not separate the practical needs related to the design of the house, the definition of minimum housing standards, from

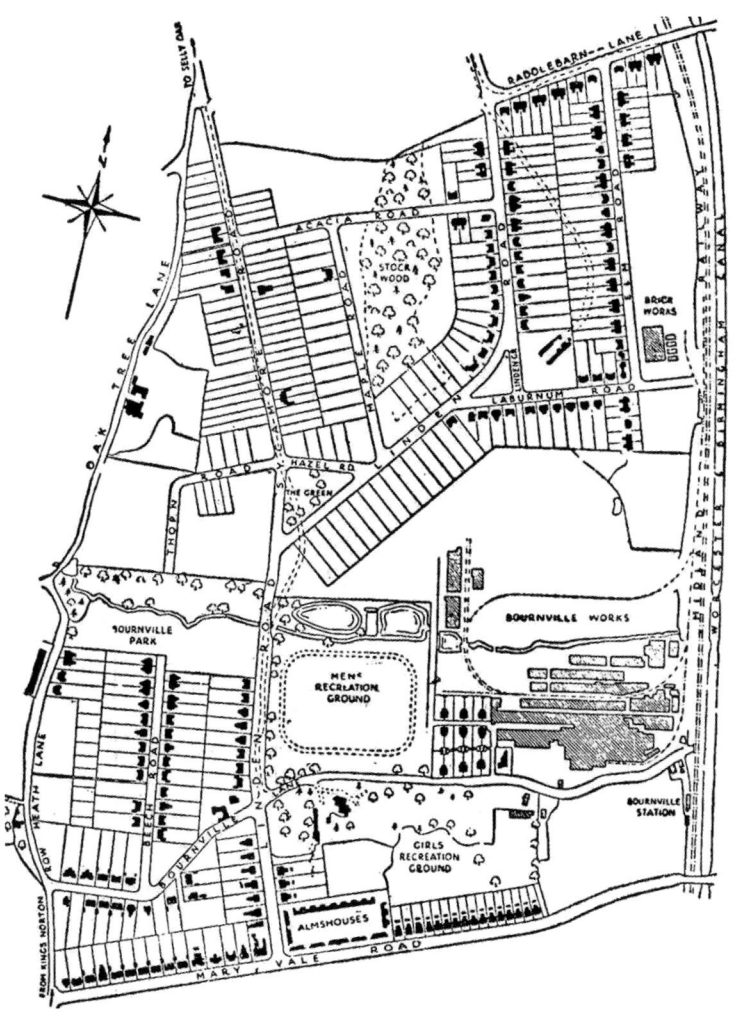

W. Alexander Harvey e A. P. Walker, Bournville planimetry
Birmingham, United Kingdom 1897
From: P.L.Giordani, L'idea della città giardino, Calderini Bologna 1962

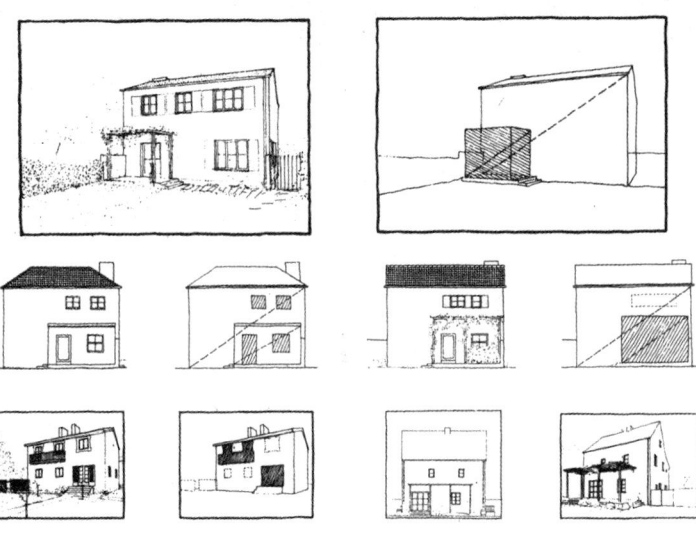

Alexander Klein, Facade studies - house, on Das Einfamilienhaus, 1934

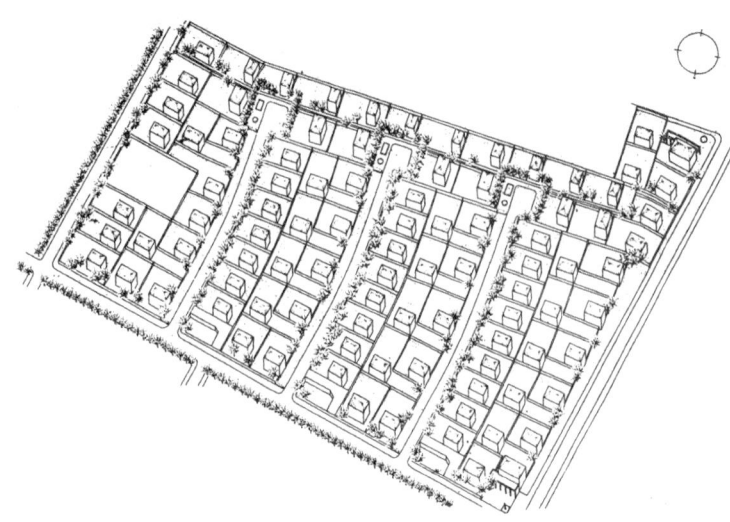

Alexander Klein, neighborhood project for the competition Heim und Garten Berlin Dahlem 1932
From: Alexander Klein - Lo studio delle piante e la progettazione degli spazi negli alloggi minimi Scritti e progetti dal 1906 al 1957- by Matilde Baffa Rivolta & Augusto Rossari, Mazzotta 1975

the needs specifically linked to architecture and identity that include particular attention to private, public and collective open spaces. This results in residential models totally alternative to the existing city or that integrate themselves with it through significant relationships. Thus the interest in the innovative redefinition of its formal and use components prevails until the first decades of the twentieth century, compared to the detached house. This redefinition stands out in projects that decisively tackle the problems resulting from new urban and social conditions. Then[9], the general shift of interest from the single-family detached house to the flat, to the aspects of self-definition and clarification of its internal features will free "the house", as Rejane Lucci says, "from that relationship with the shape of the urban ground and with the logics of occupation of that ground, with the outdoor spaces, reducing the complexity of elements and relationships that constitute the main feature of a particular urban environment"[10].

The complexity of the project experiences peculiar to the mature phase of the Modern movement clearly requires, in relation to each theme, in-depth studies. The research on the constituent elements of the "housing" to the detriment of the identity value of the "house" is presented with endless variations. The housing is intended as a reference unit infinitely repeatable in many and systematic aggregative and typological solutions useful to define new, extended residential districts designed and built near urban centres. The attention to this aspect tends to relegate to determined fields the issues related to the detached house. The result will be a range of unlimited cases in which the many aspects related to its ongoing reformulation will be addressed through in-depth analyses.

The reading of contemporary settlements of detached houses [11] gives us images of repetitive and fragmented landscapes, consisting mostly of introverted and arbitrarily individualized buildings, indifferent to the logic of contextual integration, in many cases overwhelmed by incisive infrastructure systems and territorial equipment. These settlements are often built only "on the basis of *convenient* dimensioning, calculations of efficiency, simplified dimensional ratios, technical devices with global diffusion"[12]. They are undefined fields both for the little attention paid to the formal solutions related to the individual units and their possible multiple and varied combinations, and for the inadequate importance given to the elements and relationships that constitute the main feature and the sense of belonging. These settlement areas, discontinuously developed mainly in areas adjacent to urban centres encompassing large and small rural areas, led to substantial difficulties in the urbanization and in maintaining important relationships with other residential areas, infrastructure and public spaces. For the detached house, we cannot but imagine configurations different from the contemporary one, suitable to represent the specific role acquired as a fundamental type of modernity able to fit, according to morphologically recognizable sets of elements, into the complex urban and territorial system[13].

Among the endless and varied design experiences of the contemporary scenery some are particularly interesting especially for their ability to represent, within morphologically coherent projects, both the identity value of the house and a new interpretation of the relationship building-plot-block. The latter in particular, in the sense of open block characterized by the presence of collective spaces, takes on a broader meaning and a more complete level of formal autonomy, becoming a constituent element of settlement areas with a significant degree of recognizability. In the design of detached houses (Hageneiland) by the MVRDV group [14] in Ypenburg, the overall typological scheme proposes traditional models, two-level single-family houses with double-pitched roof and grouped in a row. This is a contemporary reinterpretation of the traditional house with garden. The thirty-seven buildings, grouped in different ways, differentiated by the number of rooms, are arranged on four strips interrupted by link roads determining small subsystems-blocks consisting of two or more buildings with various units. Position and length of buildings, always ten meters deep, are never uniform. Their alignment takes place alternately on the east, west part, and sometimes in the middle. For this reason the related gardens are located, from time to time, on the front, on the back, or even on both sides. The different sizes and the "shifted" and alternate placing of buildings determine a variety of space-based solutions as well as different coating materials (wood, corrugated steel sheet, stone slabs, polyurethane panels, tiles). The corresponding colours (green, gray, blue, ocher) are incisive variations among the numerous houses. Repetitions and different combinations of residential blocks with limited sizes and vertical development characterize the project by Kazujo Seijo for the Sejima Townhouse in Tokyo. The extreme closeness of the buildings, permitted by law, emphasizes the system of solid-void relationships. The complex may appear at the same time as a single residential building or as a set of separate residences. The peculiarity of the distribution system inside the housing, including a high variability in the organization of living spaces mostly vertically connected, results in a variety of solutions for façade and related facings on the open spaces between the blocks. These spaces are strongly and deliberately landlocked, real roofless rooms,

Tony Garnier, industrial city, views of the residential with single-family building block
From: A.A.V.V., Dalle città ideali alla città virtuale - by Carlo Mezzetti, Edizioni Kappa 2005

Walter Gropius, house number 16 - Weissenhof, Stuttgart 1927, experimental neighborhood
From: Winfried Nerdinger, Walter Gropius - Opera completa, Electa 1985

MVRDV, single-family homes, Hageneiland - Ypenburg NL
Photo by Paola Branciaroli

MVRDV, Hageneiland - Ypenburg, view from top

38 Shapes & identity

SANAA Kazuyo Sejima & Associates, Seijo Town Houses
Photo by Hisao Suzuki, El Croquis n.139 2008
SANAA Kazuyo Sejima Ryue Nishizawa 2004 - 2008

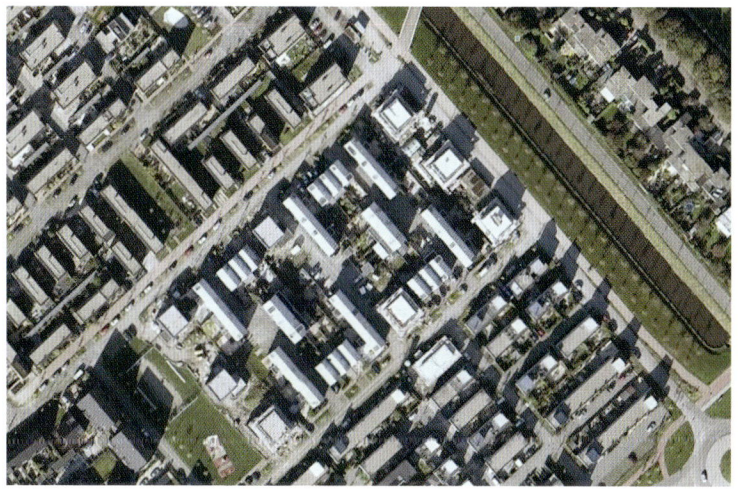

S333 Architecture + Urbanism Ltd
Bloembollenhof Vijfhuizen, NL - view from top

Rosa Branciaroli

5333, Housing, Bloembollenhof Vijfhuizen, NL

40 Shapes & identity

spaces with a greater collective connotation than others[15]. The adoption of an apparent irregularity in the arrangement and orientation of residential blocks characterizes the intervention in Vijfhuizen, (1998-2003) Haarlemmermeer, by the s333group. As in the case of the Hageneiland project by the MVRDV studio, the typological scheme of the traditional house is proposed, with a double-pitched roof, with a greater degree of variation in the aggregative systems and size of the houses[16]. The consequent building - garden spaces - collective spaces relationship is highly articulate and with a significant degree of formal identity, accentuated by the common "casing" of aluminum and wooden buildings.

In these examples taken within a very broad scenery, with particular reference to the suburban settlements, the individualized revival of the model of the detached house with garden, weak construction element of the contemporary extended suburban city, is overcome. The ongoing review implemented in these cases on the components related to the formal-identity aspect of the building analyzed in itself and according to the different hypotheses of diversification and grouping is part of a design path that highlights central issues of the detached house interpreted in itself and within the different systems of relationships characterizing the contemporary urban context.

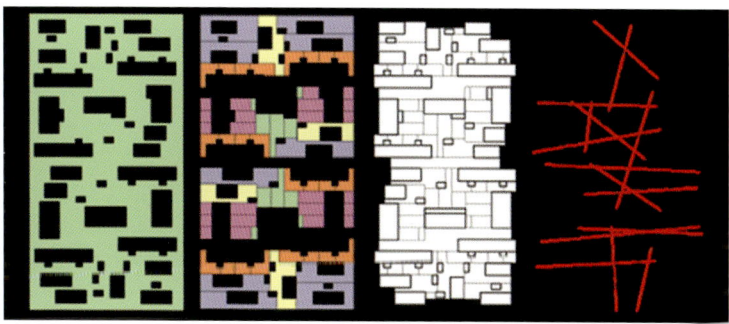

S333, Bloembollenhof Vijfhuizen, NL
Ideograms

NOTES

1. The city, Aldo Rossi states, has been largely characterized by the residence: "We can say that cities where the residential aspect was not present do not exist or did not exist. Where this aspect had a completely subordinate role in the formation of a urban element (the castle, the military camp), we soon came to a modification to the benefit of the residence". The house, Aldo Rossi maintains, representing the concrete way of living of people, the accurate manifestation of a culture, changes very slowly. "Viollet-Le Duc in his great fresco belonging to the French architecture inserted in a dictionary where every opinion is supported by the analysis of tangible facts, writes that: "in the art of architecture, the house is certainly what best characterizes the habits, tastes and customs of people, and its order, as well as its distribution, changes only in a very long time". A. Rossi, L'architettura della città - Clup

2. "... the way of dividing plots, only linked to economic problems, does not correspond to a defined way of building the house. Within any plot, we know what is the possible volume, the number of floors, if necessary, the minimum distance from the boundaries, but not the architectural aspect of the building to be built. This is how the recurrent elements of the contemporary cityscape everybody knows arise: a varied range of building types, houses without clear relationships among each other, unclear void spaces among them, debris areas as "no man's land", roads with inexplicably wider and wider sections, but with no logics and proportions with the surrounding space, and so on". Rejane Lucci, La costruzione dell'abitare – Lezioni di architettura - Cuen '91

3. "The symbolic connotation of "Levittown"'s model, thanks to the worldwide spreading of American sitcoms, will decisively affect domestic consumptions in Europe and in the western world, changing the collective imagination of the house and helping to increase the distance between common sense and "cultured architecture". Giovanni Marras, La casa isolata come standard – Mitologia versus tipologia – in: AA. La casa, Forme e ragioni dell'abitare, Skira 2008

4. "Ledoux does not make direct references (even if there are already several treatises on rural architecture). On the one hand, Laugier's theory on the primitive hut (worded to coincide with the first industrial revolution); on the other hand, Palladio's experience and the construction of the high-class house in the countryside, in front of the royal city: the Paris of the revolution with its contradictions, its size, its high density". Monestiroli A.: "Le forme dell'abitazione" (in: A. Monestiroli, L'Architettura della realtà, Clup '79)

5. A.Monestiroli: "Le forme dell'abitazione" (in: A. Monestiroli, L'Architettura della realtà, Clup '79), cit.

6. A.Monestiroli: "Le forme dell'abitazione", (in: A. Monestiroli, L'Architettura della realtà, Clup '79) .

7. "The metropolis, source of anguish for the nineteenth-century middle-class thought, is here divided into groups of *corresponding dimensions*, without denying, as in Owen and Fourier's utopias, the structural basis of the urban economy, and without wrongfully connecting, as in Sorya y Mata's model, the needs of an infrastructure development to the location of residences, markets and production sites". M. Tafuri, F. Dal Co, Ch.2, Le origini dell'urbanistica moderna – Architettura contemporanea 1, Electa.

8. Theorized in opposition to the city, the city-garden model is linked to the concept of self-sufficiency peculiar both to the supporters of the horizontal city and to those of the vertical city. The city-garden is for Howard the "third magnet", intermediate and independent element between city and countryside. "A concept of detached groups is underlined, rather than the re-

Shapes & identity

ciprocal links among districts. It will therefore be an obstacle for the overall urban organization and the growth of the city in a compact and flexible enough shape". Chiaia V., L'alternativa tipologica, Daedalus

9. The instrumental and distorted use of scientific principles related to housing developed in the final phase of the Modern era have as a generalized result the indefinite and non-place construction of residential areas close to large urban centres.

10. Rejana Lucci, La costruzione dell'abitare – Lezioni di architettura - Cuen '91, cit.

11. This particularly refers to private building of the last decades in urban areas placed outside consolidated urban centres.

12. "The search for appropriate spatial relationships (internal/external, individual/collective, public/private, architecture/nature), is overcome by types based on "convenient" dimensioning, calculations of efficiency, simplified dimensional ratios, technical devices with global diffusion". John Marras, La casa isolata come standard Mitologia versus tipologia, in: AA., La casa, Forme e ragioni dell'abitare, Skira, 2008.

13. The new technologies relating to the fundamental issues of sustainability and eco-environmental compatibility are being applied.

14. Area of urban sprawl (The Hague suburbs), an archipelago composed of numerous islands surrounded by water, MRVRDV, 1991-2002, El Croquis 111

15. Kazuyo Sejima Ryue Nishizawa Seijo Townhouse in Tokio. In SANAA 2004-2008, El Croquis n.139, 2008

16. S333 Vijfhuizen, (1998-2003) Haarlemmermeer

3
Inseparables

Massimiliano Scuderi

Flavin Barracks, Chinati Foundation, 1987,
Photo Robert Wison
Publisher: The Chinati Foundation, 1987
© 1987, by The Chinati Foundation

Sergison & Bates, Suburban Housing, 1998-2000, Stevenage (UK)

A hypothesis

Some crucial issues regarding the metadisciplinary and interdisciplinary aspects of the architectural project are often sidestepped, mainly in the academic world. The age-old problem of the autonomy of knowledge "boxes" and their inability to communicate is generally an unusual topic, although the expansion of cognitive horizons on how arts and sciences form a coalition seems more and more urgent. In a meeting with the architect Piero De Rossi, Lyotard states: *if we look at the thought of the late eighteenth century, we are surprised to see that the interdisciplinary exchanges - if we may call them so - are already a rule... the separation of disciplines, instead, is closely linked to the establishment of the modern university, roughly around 1811.*[1] This epistemological problem, that is to say, the *correspondances* among searches related to different fields of thought, especially in the preliminary stages of the development of any type of project, is generally solved through an approach based on topics seeking to reassert the gap existing among different types of knowledge - for example between technology and the humanities. This brief essay aims at formulating a principle: what each of us produces, meaning in this specific case the dwelling types of space, must arise from a knowledge and awareness process. For example, the categories of art and architecture belong to a wider discourse on the quality of meta-design thought - we can define it archetypal - which includes the concepts of place, identity and history. There is a field among the arts and other disciplines in which reality can be analyzed from multiple viewpoints, a place where knowledge, insights, culture and nature meet. In the initial phase of the creative process, the ideas are compared before being included in specific areas of knowledge and while waiting for providing the right answers to different problems.

Architects versus Artists

The relationship between architects and art has often been achieved through embezzlement and, even worse, without understanding the meaning of the creative process behind works and projects. In an essay published on Lotus[2], entitled *Two cultures*, quoted in turn from an essay by Charles Percy Snow of 1959[3], Donald Judd, father of the American minimalist movement, strictly talks about the relationship between architecture and art, arguing that *the current architecture takes advantage of the art following at least two directions. It incorporates both the shapes and the use of the materials of past and contemporary art, as well as in particular of historic architecture, and even more*

Massimiliano Scuderi

miserably, when building museums. In this sense it is significant the testimony of a Texan art dealer about Gordon Matta-Clark. In 1977 the architect Frank O'Gerhy, curious and passionate about everything was happening in the art, became interested in buying one of the photos regarding Gordon Matta-Clark projects, in particular those related to the so-called "buildings cuts", namely the intervention of the artist when literally cutting portions of buildings. Some time later, after buying a house of the twenties in Santa Monica, O'Gehry cut it into pieces and then modified and rebuilt it in a different way. Although his personal story on his hanging around with other artists was well-known, such as with Chuck Arnoldi or the artists of the *Ferus Gallery* in Los Angeles, and even though it represented a constant element in O'Gehry's life, it would not allow him to thoroughly understand the intention and the meaning of the Matta-Clark's work. In fact, the meaning of cuts and removals from the buildings by the American sculptor was reduced to a mere formal problem. In this sense it is useful to take up the thread of Donald Judd who, in the same essay, continues: *a building intended as a sculpture is a bad idea to start with, but the architects know very little about the recent history of sculpture. The imitation is so ignorant that would never find a place in top-quality art*. As evidence of the veracity of this statement, many exhibitions forcibly sought a close relationship between artists' works and architects' works. This relationship was mostly returned as coincidence of formal results, an egregious oversight that does not reflect the reality of facts. A careful analysis of the origins of shapes, visual art and architecture, would be beneficial in resolving the classic misunderstanding on the formal overlapping between the two languages. To better understand whether these correspondences really exist, it may be useful to recall the history of some pieces of research, considering as cultural context of reference the contemporary cityscape and, in particular, its most important minimum unit: the house.

Two cultures, common practices

Dan Graham, American conceptual artist, assumed that in the seventies many examples of minimalist art were born from the observation of orthogonal grids of cities and, more generally, from the survey on the American suburban landscape. In *Homes for America* he analyzed the stylistic variations of serial residential types. It is interesting if we think about the studies developed by architects such as Alexander Klein and his methods of classification of housing types. His analyses on plants and typological variations in housing projects were often read as functionalist comparisons. Instead, they imply broad

Homes for America

D. GRAHAM

Belleplain	Garden City
Brooklawn	Garden City Park
Colonia	Greenlawn
Colonia Manor	Island Park
Fair Haven	Levitown
Fair Lawn	Middleville
Greenfields Village	New City Park
Green Village	Pine Lawn
Plainsboro	Plainview
Pleasant Grove	Plandome Manor
Pleasant Plains	Pleasantside
Sunset Hill Garden	Pleasantville

Large-scale 'tract' housing 'developments' constitute the new city. They are located everywhere. They are not particularly bound to existing communities; they fail to develop either regional characteristics or separate identity. These 'projects' date from the end of World War II when in southern California speculators or 'operative' builders adapted mass production techniques to quickly build many houses for the defense workers over-concentrated there. This 'California Method' consisted simply of determining in advance the exact amount and lengths of pieces of lumber and multiplying them by the number of standardized houses to be built. A cutting yard was set up near the site of the project to saw rough lumber into those sizes. By mass buying, greater use of machines and factory produced parts, assembly line standardization, multiple units were easily fabricated.

Housing Development, over view, Bayonne, New Jersey

Housing Development, front view, Bayonne, New Jersey

"The Serenade" - Cape Coral unit, Fla.

Each house in a development is a lightly constructed 'shell' although this fact is often concealed by fake (half-stone) brick walls. Shells can be added or subtracted easily. The standard unit is a box or a series of boxes, sometimes contemptuously called 'pillboxes.' When the box has a sharply oblique roof it is called a Cape Cod. When it is longer than wide it is a 'ranch.' A

Two Entrance Doorways, "Two Homehomes", Jersey City, N.J.

two-story house is usually called 'colonial.' If it consists of contiguous boxes with one slightly higher elevation it is a 'split level.' Such stylistic differentiation is advantageous to the basic structure (with the possible exception of the split level) whose plan simplifies construction on discontinuous ground levels).

There is a recent trend toward 'two home homes' which are two boxes split by adjoining walls and having separate entrances. The left and right hand units are mirror reproductions of each other. Often sold as private units are strings of apartment-like, quasi-discrete cells formed by subdividing laterally an extended rectangular parallelopiped into as many as ten or twelve separate dwellings.

Developers usually build large groups of individual homes sharing similar floor plans and whose overall grouping possesses a discrete flow plan. Regional shopping centers and industrial parks are sometimes integrated as well into the general scheme. Each development is sectioned into blocked-out areas containing a series of identical or sequentially related types of houses all of which have uniform or staggered set-backs and land plots.

Sub-deck, Jersey City, New Jersey

The logic relating each sectioned part to the entire plan follows a systematic plan. A development contains a limited, set number of house models. For instance, Cape Coral, a Florida project, advertises eight different models:

A The Sonata
B The Concerto
C The Overture
D The Ballet
E The Prelude
F The Serenade
G The Nocturne
H The Rhapsody

Center Court, Entrance, Development, Jersey City, N.J.

In addition, there is a choice of eight exterior colors:
1 White
2 Moonstone Grey
3 Nickle

LAWN GREEN

4 Seafoam Green
5 Lawn Green
6 Bamboo
7 Coral Pink
8 Colonial Red

As the color series usually varies independently of the model series, a block of eight houses utilizing four models and four colors might have forty-eight times forty-eight or 2,304 possible arrangements.

Dan Graham, Homes for America, 1971, lithograph on paper
© 1978, by Walker Art Center, Minneapolis
HYPERLINK "http://collections.walkerart.org/item/object/5147"
http://collections.walkerart.org/item/object/5147

Sergison & Bates, Suburban Housing, 1998-2000, Stevenage (UK)

MVRDV, Balancing Barn, 2007, Suffolk (UK)
Photo by Edmund Summer

essentially formal considerations, as happens for the reflection on the strength of repetition, implicit in Heinrich Tessenow's constructive logic. In the book *Hausbau und dergleichen (Elementary Comments on Building)*[4] he states: *"Among the means available to express our feelings, the craftsman works are neither the best nor the most comfortable, but the most superficial and inexpressive. Consequently, when we want to express a strong and rich feeling in craftsman work, we always prefer to employ repetition, as the poet repeats its simple "but not" to sing his lament and despair"*[5]. Dan Graham applies the same principle in Homes for America. The in-depth analysis of serial construction methods, regarding buildings dating back to the Second World War, lets him sublimate the characteristics of standardized elements, inferring an interesting work on the origin of the American minimalist art of those years. Then, Dan Graham develops another strand of his research using a category derived from observing the traditional residential architecture, inspired by structuralist and Sartre readings: the reflected image and the problem of intersubjectivity. In Alteration to a Suburban House the layout of a typical American family space is deconstructed. The environment is thus doubled, reversed out, and the urban context is incorporated through a reflective surface, placed on the far wall of the house.

Architecture Returns Art[6]

Over the past twenty years a new current of thought developed in the architectural international scenery. There seems to be again an interest in architecture as a profession, as the practice of a knowledge linked to the building tradition. It is interesting to see how young studios are able, remaining within a specific discipline, to trigger processes of linguistic renewal of projects. What seems to be more innovative is the intrinsic quality of these productions, as in the case of Stevenage residences in Hertfordshire by the British Sergison & Bates studio. This semi-detached house is the result of a formal language hiding a great desire for representation through an apparent understatement. In addition to the inevitable references to the lessons of authors such as Heinrich Tessenow, the project manages to dialectically engage the suburban context through the use of traditional shapes, on the verge of the vernacular, combining with the language peculiar to the contemporary world. A slight *displacement* is due to the inclusion of a disturbing shape in its stigmatizing the image of domesticity, more than any other in the context. Analyzing the plan, the building is definable as a construction consisting of two symmetrical units which determine the introflexed feature of front façades and the everted feature of the two back façades, through a rotation along the axis of symmetry represented by the central spine wall. This results, with plastic, figurative and relational implications, in a sense of conviviality of the front space and a sense of privacy for the back spaces, characterized by terraces and private gardens. Although bounded by disciplinary constraints, even here it is possible to see the cultural attitude and the quality of the design procedure which put together the processuality of these architects with the intrinsic nature of the works by Gordon Matta-Clark and Dan Graham.

Intimacy

Even before the search for typological and architectural solutions, the project of a house poses general problems relating to the quality of void spaces, as a memory of other solids and voids belonging to the spaces of memory, as a reminder of features determining our personal vision of living, as an intimate, almost psychoanalytical dimension, of perceiving other qualities from the everyday space. In the two books *Non è cosa and Non siamo mai soli (It is not the case and We are never alone)*, the sociologist Franco La Cecla e Luca Vitone, Genoese artist based in Milan, discuss, in the style of Claude Levy Strauss, the relationship between material and intimate dimension of the western domestic space, returned through objects intended as specific indicators of the human existence. From the two essays it can be deduced the importance of intangible aspects of the private residence intended as an area of affection, experience and knowledge. In this sense it is interesting to remember one of the most beautiful writings by Aldo Rossi, namely *L'autobiografia scientifica*[7] *(Scientific autobiography)*, inspired by the work of the same title of 1956 by Max Planck. Precisely from this reference, in the incipit he uses the principle of permanence of human energy in buildings. It is a programmatic statement used in the book to introduce a personal working method, in which existential and cultural aspects intercept the professional ones, in an intimate and everyday practice of the profession: *"My intention has always been to write projects, stories, films, paintings, more and more independently from each technique because this identified more with the thing being at the same time a projection of reality"*[8]. In recent years, many architects have developed some design considerations taking them from the direct experience of art. A symbolic case, almost representing a turning point in recent years about the subject, is represented by Herzog & De Meuron Swiss studio - today perhaps it would be better to say global -. In an interview with Jeffrey Kipnis in the '90s[9], the two architects talked about their relationship with contemporary art and in particular with Joseph Beuys, for whom they worked in 1978 to the Feuerstatte II work. *He showed us things we had never seen before. For example, how to work with materials: he did not use them only in a mono-functional way as architects tend to do - he had a much more sensual approach and he gave symbolic meaning to materials. However, this symbolic aspect has never been part of our own work. Perhaps there is something in what you say, when you talk about the void with respect to our work.* This statement highlights the close relationship between representational arts and architecture, especially if we think about the research conducted in the sixties by artists like Vito Acconci. After abandoning the context of the galleries, they chose city and architecture as areas where to develop issues peculiar to behavioural problems and to the investigation of space. Works as *Seedbed* and

MVRDV, Balancing Barn, 2007, Suffolk (UK)
Photo by Edmund Summer

then *Following piece*, in which he daily chose to follow a person on the street until he passed from a public to a private space, allowed many generations of architects to deepen their knowledge of the socio-cultural context they worked in, until creating new and extreme types of project, as the result of a cultural approach directly borrowed from artistic experiments. A useful example is represented by a residence recently designed by the Dutch MVRDV architects in Suffolk, England. Born as a house for two people, although able to accommodate eight people, the building consists of a long longitudinal body, entirely covered with reflective metal sheet mirroring the surrounding nature. The name *Balancing Barn* is justified by the peculiarities of this architecture. It is surrealistically and half suspended on the landscape, visible from inside the house through side windows and a large glass opening cut in the floor of the living room. This climax of instability, of *no future* aesthetic[10], permeates to some extent the whole building and in general seems to be important in understanding the conceptual, symbolic and figurative value of the production of the Dutch studio and, more generally, of contemporary architecture.

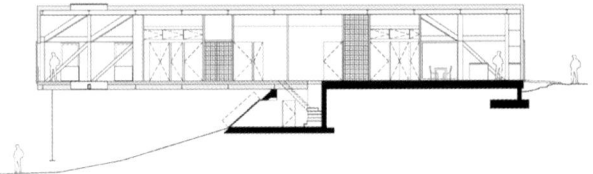

MVRDV, Balancing Barn, 2007, Suffolk (UK), longitudinal section

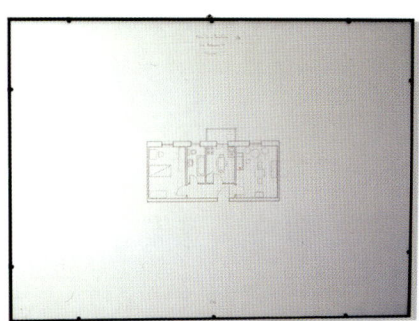

Luca Vitone, we are never alone (Metronome) 1994
Drawing, 50x70 cm, sweaters, shelf
Photo by Roberto J Marossi

NOTES

1. J. F. Lyotard, Piero Derossi, Che cosa si cerca?, in Lotus n°73, Electa, 1992, Milano.

2. D. Judd, "Two cultures" in: Lotus International: *Dopo la capanna decorata / After the Decorated Shed*, n° 73, 1992, pp. 119-125.

3. C.P. Snow, *The Two Cultures and the Scientific Revolution* - Rede Lecture, Cambridge University Press, 1959. The essay focuses on the problem of the relationship between science and the humanities.

4. H. Tessenow, *Hausbau und dergleichen*, B. Cassirer, Berlin, 1916

5. In the chapter about order, the autor quotes the following poem to explain the effectiveness of repetition: «everything is dark, everything is misty, when my love is not with me, I thought she loved me, but no, but no, but no, but no, she hates me».

6. The title of this section refers to the book by Luciano Fabro, *Arte Torna Arte*, Einaudi, 1999, Milano

7. Fabro, Arte Torna Arte, Einaudi, 1999, Milano.

8. A. Rossi, *Autobiografia scientifica*, Pratiche editrice, 1990, Parma.

9. J. Kipnis, *A conversation with Jacques Herzog*, in El croquis n° 04, El Croquis editorial, 1997, Madrid.

10. This is how the nihilistic vision of the world of the punk movement of the seventies and eighties is defined.

4

The single-family house from the garden city to the urban sprawl

Carlo Pozzi

Montesilvano: residential urban growth
Photo by Paolo De Stefano
From Piano territoriale della provincia di Pescara, Grafica Siva, Montesilvano 1999

58 The single-family house from the garden city to the urban sprawl

This reflection applies to the mid-Adriatic coast, from the Pescara urban scale to expand to a urban system meant to tie Pescara and Chieti with the small centres revolving around the cities. The urban scale also tends to spread parallel to the coast, predicting the birth of a city out of all proportions, characterized by indefinite dimensions. This investigation consists of two parts, each divided into three short chapters. The first section deals with the tradition of small houses that shaped the city and the Adriatic coast in the early part of the twentieth century, showing fragments of a hypothetical garden city. The second part extends to include the urban phenomena of the late twentieth century, characterized by *densification* and *sprawl*. Finally, we will try to reflect on the prospects of the ongoing research.

First part (of the twentieth century)

"The gradual increase in density, the manifestation of buildings for rent and the progressive disappearance of the single-family house, the transformation of the open block into closed isolated block, etc... The process of construction and transformation is similar to many others which took place anywhere in the capitalist world. So the process destroys **a certain gracefulness** *showed by the first small middle-class city and it fully adapts to the needs of capitalist speculation".*
(A. Renna, L'illusione e i cristalli. Immagini di architettura per una terra di provincia, Clear, Roma 1980)

- *South Pescara: the Aurum and the Pineta houses.*

The group of houses dating back to the '20s and '30s is arranged between the Pineta and the sea, having as its settlement heart, since the first parcelling-out, the former Kursaal, then the Aurum and then one of the few monuments of the city. It is a very important example for a contemporary reflection on the ways of living.

The small surviving houses support the statement that *"the single-family detached house represents one of the real and possible alternatives to the problem of living"* (A. Renna, L'illusione e i cristalli, Clear, Roma 1980) and evoke that *gracefulness* almost lost due to the massive densifications that transformed this urban area as well.

On the one hand, the strategy of urban planning, on the other, the features of a period of artistic and architectural culture, transformed this small district of low-rise houses among the pine trees into a complex in which uniformity and regularity in size and density have very diverse formal results, although delimited in the specific language of an era. The general standard (coverage ratio of 1/2 with the use of the front open area as a garden, and back area for bathroom and garage) has been interpreted and "changed" from time to time by the couple dweller-designer, by the individual choices for the place of residence, within the great eclectic decorative scenery which proposed the different currents of Liberty and Floreale style, rather than of Art Nouveau and Vienna Secession. We are not interested here in identifying the individual stylistic aspects, because, moreover, the effects in the province are never so bright and immediately identifiable. Rather, we want to offer a framework for a better understanding of the phenomenon. The "march to the Pineta" operation actually started in 1910 with the Liberi Plan, after the name of its designer, the engineer who was designing the Politeama Aternino (then Teatro Michetti), the Kursaal (later the Aurum) and some houses in the same plot. Besides his undoubted talent, this great planning activity is probably also due to the relationship with the poet D'Annunzio. After masterfully celebrating the Versilia pine forests, the poet refused to be co-opted in his native city, abruptly rejecting the donation of a large plot from the municipality so that he could build a house there and come back to live in Pescara. *"I do not want neither temporal nor spiritual gifts. I am self-sufficient and I live where I like in the houses I choose"* (R. Colapietro, Pescara 1860-1960, Costantini, Pescara, 1980).

The Liberi Plan drew a harmonious district of small houses, gardens, tree-lined avenues in the Pineta and towards the sea. The Kursaal was the central point of the plan and it remained so only on the floor area when it became liqueur distillery in 1919. In this way, it also gained force as "urban monument" after the addition of the horseshoe section, designed by Michelucci, with the possible role of a link among the district, the Pineta and the city.

The plan divided the area into 52 800-1000 square meter islets at the minimum distance of 40 meters from the sea, each divided into several building plots. The boundaries of the individual areas were defined according to very strict rules, aiming at overcoming the individualistic and privatistic attitude carried out by the parcelling-out mechanism itself. In October 1910, according to the Development Plan, 32 building plots were assigned to the Rione Pineta, obliged to build within a year, but after fourteen months only 15 plots were partly paid and the first small villa was built in only one of them. Liberi launched the idea of a **garden city**: wide avenues, the park, the stadium, the pavil-

La Porta Villa
Photo by Carlo Pozzi

ion for exhibitions, schools, a few areas in the pine forest for playing. The goal was to transform the Pineta d'Avalos in a health seaside resort, with a more comprehensive redevelopment plan regulating the building industry.The idea of the garden city finds in the inter-war European city examples of social housing built by Rationalism, characterized by precision, architectural uniformity and sometimes by a monotonous repetition. Here, as well as in other cities on the Adriatic coast, the garden city is expressed as the manifestation of economic prosperity with the construction of a status symbol.

The middle-class clients of that period wanted small villas rich in "distinctive" elements, decorations sometimes richer than the house itself, its installations and its distributive features. Small houses with a small garden, son of the Mediterranean pine forest, among and on whose "chiappini" (forests) sits Pescara, a typological similar pattern and then a flurry of decoration. The houses have a raised ground floor according to the standard, someone has a basement, many have only one floor, others two, some a small tower - roof-terrace.

All usually elaborate Liberty-style decorative themes, with a different emphasis on the elements. However, the tone remains quiet, far from the artistic and sculptural vagaries of the Catalan Modernism or the Secession graphic virtuosity. Small brick houses with overhanging roofs and decoration strips remain on the background.

Their real richness lies in the constant dialogue with the Pineta and the sea, varying a few elements among the repeated ones, with the symphonic effect of a score, where the whole is worth more than all the flickering individual expressive moments.

- North Pescara: railmen houses, small villas on the Riviera

The 1882 Expansion Development Plan, commonly known as Muzi because it was prepared by the engineer Tito Altobelli under Leopold Muzi administration, located the railmen houses along Umberto I Main Street, as it was the avenue moving from the station to the sea and therefore near the working area.

In addition, the 1981 Contest for the railway station debris area included in the announcement the demand for new railmen houses in the central area. But precisely this focus created a different kind of speculative expectations for such areas, then as today. For this reason the social housing houses were moved to a northern suburban plot, where the value of land was obviously much lower.The expropriation took place between 1921 and 1922 and covered 4,000 square meter sandy shores belonging to Mr. Antonio Sabucchi. He accepted the transaction on condition that the main road of the new housing settlement was named after him, from the sea to the garden of the villa, later demolished and whose park became public.

The project was drawn up by the engineers Benedetto Sorge and Tommaso Piccirilli. Then, a 1,200 square meter area was divided to be donated to Penne bishop to build Sant'Antonio church. It assumed the role of monumental element, out of scale compared to the size of the small residential groupings.

The district was born in 1921 thanks to the "Casa Nostra" Co-operative Society, created by railmen. The project was developed around the main axis, characterized by a pine tree-lined central reservation. The five fractions of land resulting from the crosses with Regina Margherita Avenue, Regina Elena Avenue and Riviera Avenue are divided into fenced plots where there are three different building types (A, B, C). In one part of the area between Regina Margherita Avenue, Sabucchi Avenue and Riviera Avenue there is a playground. The buildings are designed as belonging to affordable housing, but the decorative elements denote a particular attention for the stylistic trends of the time, in the definition of planked basements, in the window frames and entrance doors, in the corner loggias based on columns, in gratings of small balconies.

If railmen houses are "moved" from the centre to what were then the outskirts, the most central front façade of the city on the Adriatic, in particular the stretch from Umberto Main Street to Zanni roundabout, is characterized by a series of detached buildings intended as manor houses or sometimes as small buildings. Their presence still has a strongly evocative aspect, despite the replacements of the '60s and '70s with high-density and no quality speculative housing, whose development has profoundly altered the **"waterline" of the city into the sea**, covering the "bathing" aspect thanks to which, in the post-war reconstruction, Piccinato cherished the idea of a higher density urban area towards the interior, sloping down to the sandy shore.

Even here the structure of a smart parcelling-out remains to some extents caught in the deep changes the city underwent especially in its architectural image. From Umberto Main Street almost to Leopoldo Muzi Street, a double row of plots runs along the Riviera with a quincunx staggering so as to allow the single-family house lying behind to watch the sea and sometimes to access it through an independent path. Now, on those plots tall buildings hardly reveal the underlying order that also shows the webs of topography, with yellowed tax maps.

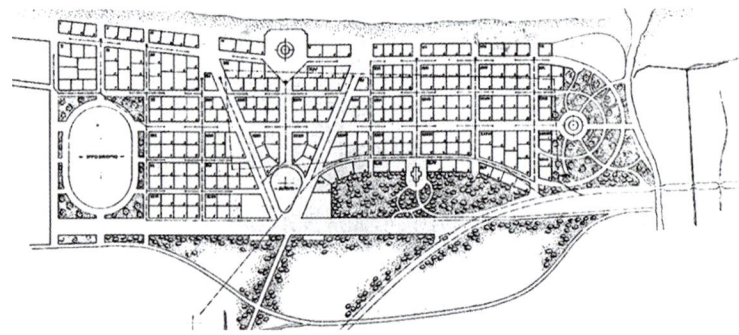

Plan of neighborhood designed by A. Liberi
Sistema di archiviazione Faidata (consulenza D. Colalongo)
dal libro di C. Bianchetti, Pescara, Laterza, Bari-Roma 1997

Railroader housing, Pescara
Photo by Carlo Pozzi

64 The single-family house from the garden city to the urban sprawl

- Villas on the mid-Adriatic coast

When bathing in the seawater was not yet in fashion and the coasts were still hostile and in some cases to be reclaimed, the great villas of landowners settled in a back position compared to the shoreline. However, they used a piece of land of considerable size as an extended strip that from the foot of the hill would reach the beach, representing in this way a section interpreting the geomorphology of the mid-Adriatic coast.

It happened to the villas today incorporated in the Pescara area. A few fragments remain of these villas, such as parts of buildings, parts of the park, evidences of the road shaded by a double row of pine trees leading to the sea: Sabucchi Villa and Muzi Villa. A heap of rubble ignored within a public park remain of Sabucchi Villa, site of the legendary overnight stay of King Vittorio Emanuele II.

Muzi Villa was complex on a urban scale. It was established as a rural unit including the manor house, the rural residence, the area for services and work, the chapel (the only well-preserved artifact of popular devotion). An industrial section with buildings for work, the furnace, the residences of the workers, in a sort of phalanstère for autonomous parts related to the territory, were then added to the rural part. These parts, too, were affected by the rapid and disrespectful growth of Pescara. Something similar also happened to the villas on the coast just north of Pescara (Silvi, Pineto, Roseto), which suffered similar phenomena of interruption with the sea, even more than what happened to the opposite twentieth-century residential urbanizations, the construction of the coastal railway first, the Adriatic main road then, and finally the most recent avenues of the Riviera.

The villas perched on the hill, Basile Villa and Mezzopreti Villa, were more intact. After all, their view of the sea was not affected. For these **"Adriatic houses"** the references range from Palladian distributive approaches to eclectic solutions of various kinds and styles. It is the period that from the "fin de siècle" (for large territorial villas) to the opening of the new (for urban villas) acts as a precondition for modernity. In the province, as always, and along the Adriatic coast, nothing is invented and from the eclectic and academic references to the Renaissance, you pass to the Catalan Modernism and Liberty style, intertwining quotations by Olbrich with quotations by the first Behrens, loans from Moretti Neomedievalism to the redesign of the Guimard phytomorphic arabesques for naturalistic parapets. The middle-class taste is directed towards new exotic paths, towards an "art collage" house, objects with a "poetic reaction", through the use of flower decorations, to add symbolic meanings to small single-family houses, sometimes devoid of in-depth typological analyses and a bit ordinary. In this sense, some elements characterizing our small houses, even more than large villas, but with the interchange and return from one another, suffer from a condition typical of an age squeezing even the last possible relationship with tradition, before the protesting outbreak of the avant-gardes and the subsequent excessive power of modernity.

And so, starting from the book "Curvatura delle linee dell'architettura antica" (Curved lines in ancient architecture) (1884) and reading history in its own way, Basile promotes the charm of the Nordic castle *"without barycentre"* and *"shaken by an inner suffering. The castle is miniaturized gathering together in a modest mass all its fundamental features"* (M. Nicoletti, L'architettura Liberty in Italia, Laterza, Bari): curved staircases, basement, semi-hexagonal or hexagonal bow-windows on corbels, overhanging roofs on brackets and especially small towers that become a fundamental element of that period (at least for Basile, Sommaruga, D'Aronco).

This tendency to elevate a part of the house, albeit small, is already present in the eclectic villas on the coast north of Pescara, but in the history of rural houses on the Adriatic it finds much more solid elements of reference, compared to transient linguistic reasons. One just could think about the elevation of rural houses with tower in the north of Bari, built to dominate and control the fields, about all *"the story of the farms with a tower, especially in Fasano or Salento territory"* (C. Wells - S. D'Alessandro, Alba Domenica. Masserie pugliesi, Palomar, Bari 2007), about the dovecotes of Abruzzian and Vasto rural architecture.

The small tower - dovecote - roof-terrace is therefore nothing but an element that allows the house, even more the small two-floor single-family house, to see far away and be seen from afar. This is a role always played by towers and steeples for the hundred cities of this country.

This aspect appears in some villas on the North Riviera of Pescara, sometimes in the middle of the house, sometimes as a side tower, other times summing up the whole building, projected on the other side of the road, to reach the sea: Rosa Villa, Bucci Grossi Villa, the small Scaccioni Villa, Forcella di Pilotti Villa.

Roberto Liberatoscioli, posing Pescara, Carsa Edizioni, Pescara 1999

Second part (of the twentieth century and the new millennium)

"Maybe not finished, maybe already degraded, maybe illegal, the houses are piled up along the Adriatic coast, they are narrowly lined up on absurdly straight side streets, they invade the interior, wider on the slopes of the hills, more dense in the valleys. At times, they almost reach the interior villages. The houses become shops, restaurants, factories, offices, schools. The houses become houses. And this is even more strange, because these houses do not seem made to be inhabited. Not always, at least. (...)

What thickens along the Adriatic in continuous lines is perhaps the raw material of a future, unique city. Or maybe, instead, it is the residual part, the waste material, wreckage from a time of accelerated and wasteful development". (P. Avarello, In due tappe e due percezioni, in "Le città immaginate. Un viaggio in Italia", XVII Triennale, Electa, Milano 1987)

- *The Città Sant'Angelo enclave*
"There is a general trend toward fenced communities. (...) The first question buyers make is whether it is a protected community. The demand for fenced houses is three times higher than that for not fenced houses". (M. Davis, City of Quartz: Excavating the Future in Los Angeles, Verso, London, 1990).

Fifteen years ago the Iper shopping centre landed heavily at the foot of the hill leading to Citta Sant'Angelo, near the Pescara Nord motorway exit, changing the road system for its own use and generating a section/enclave for other large shopping centres one inevitably has to cross to go to the city centre. The road climbs up through different, but recurrent situations, in a sort of return from rural to urban and vice versa: fragments of houses, villas, new residential *enclaves*. Settlements of buildings, with some architectural pretensions, located on the top of the hill overlooking the Adriatic, enclosures such as villas, small villages in the countryside protected by their being isolated and urban at the same time.

These perfect districts with their gates, electronically controlled on the access road, show, starting with legitimate concerns about the security from a widespread crime, the trend towards a social segregation also of not particularly well-off classes. They simply show the will of the "citizen-owner" not to participate anymore with his house to the urban life, not to build and inhabit the city.

It is a strange revenge of the compact city which exports one of its most successful housing types in a former steep rural area. The building is installed with no concern for a place which is totally inadequate, requiring excavation of the ground, concrete massive walls, steep streets. It is the revenge on the single-family house that so deeply altered its features through legal parcellings-out and illegal buildings, expanding the city in a thousand of branches of urban sprawl invading the territory, mixing urban and rural features, boasting the mix as immersion in nature of individual and as much as possible "designer" houses.

Traces of rural settlements chaotically emerge among the turns of the new conurbation on the hillside of Città Sant'Angelo. They declare their presence through some ruins or some farmhouses still in operation, a cultivated field and the road running through it, sometimes now used to connect two recent residential enclaves. Other fragment/enclave is Coppa Villa. After having sold most of its land to the "Moloch" Iper, it tries to find the Adriatic between trees and houses, and catches sight of it beyond the recent settlements that first separated it from the sea and then surrounded it. The juxtaposition of such different settlement areas also leads to an interesting tension, with the data from the memory running through ideas for the contemporary project. Not remaining confined and entangled in a regressive nostalgia, they build as many **"songlines"** sometimes appearing elusive. In the end they are only possible threads of a plot of positive co-presences, of overcoming the conflict by living in it, of multiple orders in the disorder: this possibility lies in the quality of the project.

- *Montesilvano: type section of the mid-Adriatic coastal city*
  "In early November 1988, on the Bologna-Pescara train there was the nineteen year old Antò Lu Purk, wearing a black turtleneck, needlecord pants, a suede jacket trimmed with dark brown wool.
  Outside the landscape passed on, reminding him of children constructions, where certain pieces looked like they had been arranged at random, just out of the box: petrol stations, suburban car showrooms, shopping centres with pennons and flags of purchasing consortia fluttering in the wind, small Public Safety barracks spacing out small groups of low-rise houses, gardens with dusty oleanders at the edge of the railwa". (S. Ballestra, Compleanno dell'iguana, Mondadori, Milan 1991).
  Like Ballestra and Avarello believe, it seems that the heap of urban sprawl is fully evaluable just passing through it along the Adriatic railway.With the speed of the train and without paying attention to driving one's car, one will realize that the Adriatic city is made of **accumulation of heterogeneous materials** at least in the road section from Rimini to Pescara.
  The first impression is all pretence: the single-family houses, in a single plot or in a sequence of plots, always seem to have something to imitate, looking for a sort of cinematographic language, in an unstable equilibrium going from Spaghetti Western Texas to Cinecittà, from its papier-mâché replicas to the varnished wooden houses by Seaside, with Central European quotations with rather singular needles and decorations, referring to Hogwarts castle, the school of magic in the Harry Potter films. This Mediterranean-style claim is only a pretence, characterized by depressed arches looking awkwardly for history, and contradicted by the large eaves of the roofs, by huge and extended balconies

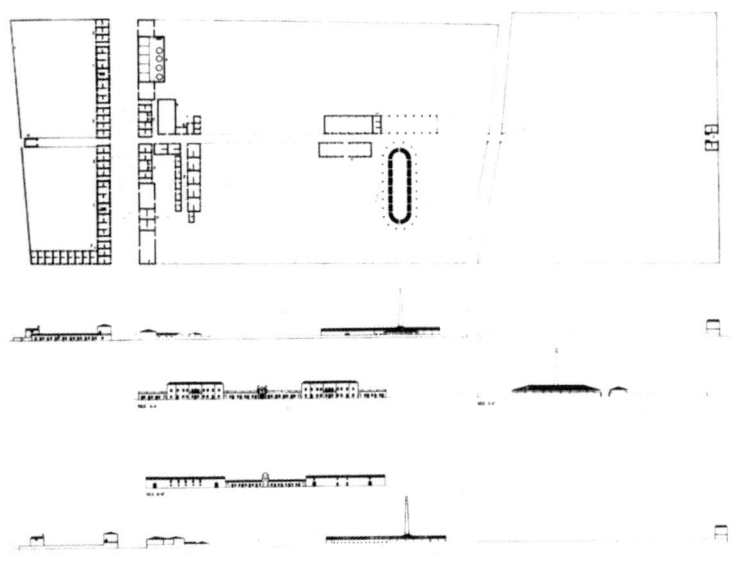

Villa Muzii, Pescara
Degree Thesis, by R. Del Nunzio, F. Riccetti
(redaction G. Grassi), dal libro di A. Renna,
Le illusioni e i cristalli, Clear, Roma 1980

(very much desired by companies), by great shelters. As a matter of fact, rather than looking for a language, there is an endless attempt to gain more space than the volume allowed by the planning instrument.so one does without the garden, one gives up the observance of distances. The walls retaining slight gradients are sometimes more impacting than the small house that tends to turn into a building. The basement, probably illegal, is first masked with an embankment, later removed when the abuse is amended or tolerated.

The Casa plan, recently and contradictorily passed, probably intercepts these instances of continuous growing of single-family houses. Regarding the materials, the structure is always made of reinforced concrete, the finishings determine the epoch of belonging of the building and may allow at least a chronological classification, ranging from the period of exposed reinforced concrete to quartz plaster, scratch-effect plastic coating, "small bricks", tile roofing used to absorb any edge object.An authentic catalogue of materials and oddities: this is what the architecture without quality project is, without architects disposed to think about a single building or on an urban scale. These architects are sometimes requested just to "sign" separate residential realities as happened a couple of decades ago in the Bari Alto discussed intervention, with the involvement of the finest minds of the time, from Aldo Rossi to Carlo Aymonino.

"Living exclusivity. The abandonment of conformity and social uniformity is the Bari Alto potential expression. The artistic challenge of well-known architects expresses in eight different styles the desire for a life characterized by the best. (...) Living safety. The sophisticated security structures, the intelligent anti-intrusion system with 24-hour video control circuits guarantee a peaceful life oriented to the natural need for living one's own privacy. (...) Bari Alto represents the authentic style for anyone who decides to give something back to life". (Bari Alto, Qualità della vita, Pubblicità immobiliare privata, Bari, 1993).

- Francavilla as Los Angeles
The lost vocation of a different Pescara, that utopian hope for a garden city identified by the first hypotheses of Piccinato's post-war reconstruction, sees a still consistent attempt with the next construction of the Villaggio Alcione council houses by Ina Casa. But moving slightly southward, along the coast and entering the domain of Francavilla al Mare, that hypothesis of hoped city is returned altered by the grotesque and absurd context, with houses of the consistency of a fairy tale (Hansel and Gretel? Sugar loaf? Marzipan?) directly built on the shoreline. In

fact, with a dream image they wanted to mask the realism of the speculative and anti-ecological operation that led Francavilla to move towards the beach, privatizing it, building artifacts furnished with the fragments of a concrete modernity scattered in the small garden: a garage, Snow White and the seven Dwarfs, the fountain that regularly does not work. The Anglo-Saxon model of the single-family house has been (badly) copied as the aspiration to free from an unsuccessful collective way of life within the residential hypothesis proposed by the Modern era: from the Unitè d'habitation in Marseille by Le Corbusier to the one kilometer and a half building left alone in the landscape of the Roman countryside in Corviale. *"Laing (...) after his arrival at the apartment building soon recognized the extraordinary number of thinly veiled antagonisms around him. (...) Never far below the froth of professional gossip was a hard mantle of personal rivalry. (...) The previous six months had been a period of continuous bickering among his neighbours, of trivial disputes over the faulty elevators and air-conditioning, inexplicable electrical failures, noise, competition for parking space. (...) The underlying tensions among the residents were remarkably strong, damped down partly by the civilized tone of the building, and partly by the obvious need to make this huge apartment block a success. (..) Soon after nine o'clock that evening, an electrical failure temporarily blacked out the 9th, 10th and 11th floors. Looking back on this episode, Laing was surprised by the degree of confusion during the fifteen minutes of the blackout. Some two hundred people were present on the 10th floor concourse, and many were injured in the stampede for the elevators and staircases. A number of absurd but unpleasant altercations broke out in the darkness between those who wanted to descend to their apartments on the lower levels and the residents from the upper floors who insisted on escaping upwards into the cooler heights of the building"*. (J. G. Ballard, High Rise, Cape, London 1975).

It has become easy and inevitable to watch with interest the deformations created here, interpreting them as "new ways of living", places of the nomadic thought and urban crossing, *"a constructive reality closer to the techniques for installation, bathing setting up and in general for the ephemeral than to those of the durable and permanent"*. (P. Desideri, La città di latta. Favelas di lusso, autogrill, svincoli stradali e antenne paraboliche, Costa & Nolan, Genova 1995).

These houses were inhabited by a metropolitan type person who lives in the urban sprawl in Francavilla and in Los Angeles. Besides, a few decades before Pescara had been compared to Chicago given its massive infrastructures and in particular considered how the freeway

Villa on the sea in Francavilla
Photo by Carlo Pozzi

Buildings on the hill of Montesilvano
Photo by Carlo Pozzi

landed on the pillars in the city right in front of the ruins of Bourbon Fortress. After the recent discoveries made by the archaeologist Andrea Staffa, we can add it leaned on the ruins of the Roman port. These houses are also interpreted as capable of freeing the individual creative experience, giving back an artistic dimension to architecture.

"In architecture we experience the outcome of the artistic experiences of the '60s in their aestheticization of the bad and the reject, with the obvious novelty, compared to the prophetic data, the concept of 'instability' introduced through volume/perspective effects and sense of movement within the buildings, and the concept of 'banality' as attention to the 'reduction' and the interpretation of the individual aspect of acting. (G. Mondaini, Abitare dopo il Moderno. Dalla casa esatta alla casa adatta, attraversando i materiali della tipologia, Sala, Pescara 2001).

It is a more artistic house the individual almost draws on himself, by modeling volumes and spaces, like a dress that fits like a glove, while the modern hypotheses were all too tight. Could this aesthetic intentionality of citizens and designers be educated or addressed towards a particular direction by the school of architecture? Could they try to build a real relationship with contemporary art?

This **claim of the ugly** (commonly understood) as an art form, went through the avant-gardes of Arte Povera, all in all so far away from architecture. They would get close to that claim, teaching something fundamental to architects, only reacting with the land, with the landscape, in the successful experience of Land Art.Through this research, the architecture has paid attention to the sign, the site, a small drop, up to shamanic bio-architecture, also proposing sensational second thoughts, and returning to the quality of urban studies:

"After years of intense and sometimes heated debate around the theme of transformation of the idea of the city, we are now facing a far too redundant "legitimation" of urban sprawl by experts. On the contrary, I believe that is why now it is time to carry out an urgent in-depth study and to distance from a too standardized and often unprofessional sympathy devoted to the phenomenon of spontaneous cities and to the misunderstanding related to the planning intervention strategies in these territories. (...) The time for provocation has finished, (...) I think it is urgent to reintroduce urban planning or, more generally, the relationship between architecture and context". (P. Desideri, Ri-comporre: una scuola italiana, prefazione a "G. Mondaini, Ri-Composizioni. Temi e figure per conversioni urbane", Gangemi, 2008)

- What architecture and what context, one would wonder...

In the construction of guidelines on the issue of enhancing the existing architectural heritage, one of the most interesting results of the inter-university research (Pescara, Ascoli Piceno, Venice) is "Opere pubbliche e città adriatica" (Public Works and the Adriatic city). The possibility of reversing the relationship between architecture and context lies among the analytical- planning actions:

"We must change the point of view employed to investigate the relationship between architecture and context. It is not that architecture must satisfy the so-called environmental preexisting features; the architecture itself must create shape in the context. If this flow of relationships has been interrupted, it is necessary to reactivate it".(C. Pozzi, La Costruzione dell'Agenda degli Indirizzi, in "Hyperadriatica" (a cura di P. Barbieri), List, Barcellona 2009).

Beyond provocations and belated conversions, it becomes urgent to reconsider the single-family house thoroughly built as the core element of the middle Adriatic urban sprawl, including authorized parcellings-out and individual initiatives (the spontaneous or informal city of the favelas has nothing to do with this...), as the fabric of the new 250-300 kilometer city that extends along the Adriatic coast, similarly, at least as aspiration, more to Miami than Chicago and Los Angeles.

This residential plot is amorphous even today. Its transformation waits for new occasions, for the planning possibility of reviving on a metropolitan scale (it is no longer a slogan) the relationship between urban and collective buildings, by enabling ecological short circuits between the pre-existing architectures (especially the public ones of the Fascist period or the first post-war reconstruction) and infrastructure networks capable of a cross communication and thus dialoguing with the natural ceiling of the hills now in the shadow, of the valleys penetrating inside, of the sea.

The three writings of the first part were published in the monographic issue "L'Architettura. Cronache e Storia", dedicated in 2003 to Pescara and the metropolitan area, edited by Carlo Pozzi and Rosario Pavia.The first text of the second part is taken from "Compresenze Adriatiche", published in "M. Del Vecchio, C. Pozzi, Ricognizioni urbane, Sala, Pescara, 1997". These short essays are now presented, largely reworked, within new research prospects.

New centrality architectures
From Hyperadriatica (by P. Barbieri), List, Barcellona 2009

Corviale building
Photo by Carlo Pozzi

NOTE

- I tre scritti della prima parte erano stati pubblicati nel numero monografico de "L'Architettura. Cronache e Storia" dedicato nel 2003 a Pescara e l'area metropolitana, curato da Carlo Pozzi e Rosario Pavia.

- Il primo testo della seconda parte è stralciato da Compresenze Adriatiche, pubblicato in "M. Del Vecchio, C. Pozzi, Ricognizioni urbane, Sala, Pescara, 1997".

- Questi brevi saggi vengono oggi presentati, in buona parte rielaborati, all'interno di una nuova prospettiva di ricerca.

5

Conurbations & detached houses

Rosa Branciaroli

Montesilvano - settlement system
In The heritage: new centrality - Hyperadriatica (byPepe Barbieri), List Barcellona 2009

The condition and specificity of the territories belonging to the current city can be interpreted considering features and conditions of the existing settling geographies, recognizing in them particular connotative elements. The attention to the settlement areas peculiar to urban suburbs highlights the aspects of greatest non-definition and complexity of the contemporary city. Grown up in fragments, discontinuously lying on weak road networks, often overwhelmed by infrastructures and services on a territorial scale, the suburbs in the polycentric- extended city characterize a large part of the contemporary landscape. The suburbs undoubtedly represent a fundamental field of investigation and application for the architectural and urban project. Although there are obvious differences related to specific cases, it is possible to recognize some common aspects and problems which tend to constantly recur. In the suburbs the urban fabric tends to fray, "it expands and opens with no apparent structure", losing the characteristic of "continuum" of the city, peculiar to the elements composing it"[1]. In the city with many centres scattered in an area without limits, the suburban settlements can be interpreted through a coherent vision as "internal parts" constituting the entire urbanized area. These parts need to be reformulated taking into account, on a differentiated scale, the systems of relationship both with the context of belonging and with the whole territorial area of reference.[2] Taking into consideration the urban area of Pescara, it is interesting to refer to the condition of the suburban "Fontanelle" settlement area and to dwell on the problems related to the detached house that strongly characterize the area.

In general, it can be stated that in the Pescara conurbation the strong impact determined by the infrastructure system - railroad, freeway, linear systems, port facilities, airports - highlights a clear opposition between spaces of mobility and spaces of residentiality, a contrast that ignores an appropriate level of contextual integration.

This is detectable to a greater extent in the suburban-extended valley and hill-foot settlements, beyond the consolidated urban system. The set of mobility networks, the equipment and services on a territorial scale coexist with the fragmented residential areas, largely overlapping with them through a difficult relationship, devoid of significant and recognizable interconnections. The overlapping trace routes of large and medium-sized facilities with the weak identity of the places in the suburban-extended city emphasizes the gap between the two parallel conditions, one peculiar to the infrastructure system, with an autonomous logic and circumscribed specialization, and one peculiar to the context, in which the reference systems of the settlement hierarchy are associated mostly with the "location" and the design of road systems, backing the fragmented settlement area. The ordinary uniformity involving building types and public and infrastructure spaces of the suburban settlement badly matches with the contemporary social potentials expressed by the whole "geography" of the places and the new economic and social structures.

The peripheral urban area, characterized by a large-scale infrastructure system, as well as by the unresolved and undefined coexistence between residential buildings and commercial and industrial structures, does not express anything meaningful and recognizable as far as the morphological aspect is concerned. In particular, any order signs can be identified except for those coming from the old and new trace routes, large expanses of open areas. There is a general relationship between the built and the natural landscape, completely different from the urban one.[3] The Fontanelle area in Pescara, a former rural area, is located south of the riverfront Tiburtina system and separated from it by a sizeable strip of commercial and industrial buildings. Bordered on the hillside by Tirino Street and by the first hills of the valley of the Pescara river it can be intended as a hybrid area, included within a context with which it maintains a few relationships except for those related to the major road layouts. Among them, the suburban elevation of the ring road touches the northern part of the area, emphasizing the division from the public residential settlements built from the sixties onwards. In the overall context of the suburbs south of the Pescara river, S. Donato and Aternum districts are the only residential settlements recognizable as a unit, even though badly connected between each other and compared to the surrounding private residential context. For these areas, the existing and newly built road layouts represent, on the whole, the urban elements of major reference and identification. The city of the past fifty years has "expanded" in general through a gradual extension of its roads that in the majority of cases prevail on all the other urban elements. "If the settling importance of the infrastructures is the hidden support system of the consolidated city, it becomes visible and physically prominent in the suburbs and the dispersed city, so much so that the reference systems of the settlement hierarchy of these areas depend on the position and the quality of its apparent design"[4].

    The almost total lack of recognizable public spaces is also frequent in the Fontanelle area as a fundamental characteristic, as well as in many similar cases. Spaces without hierarchies, differentiated only by usage, open spaces "embezzled" to the built areas, spaces which are not designed, not interpreted through significant contextual relationships.

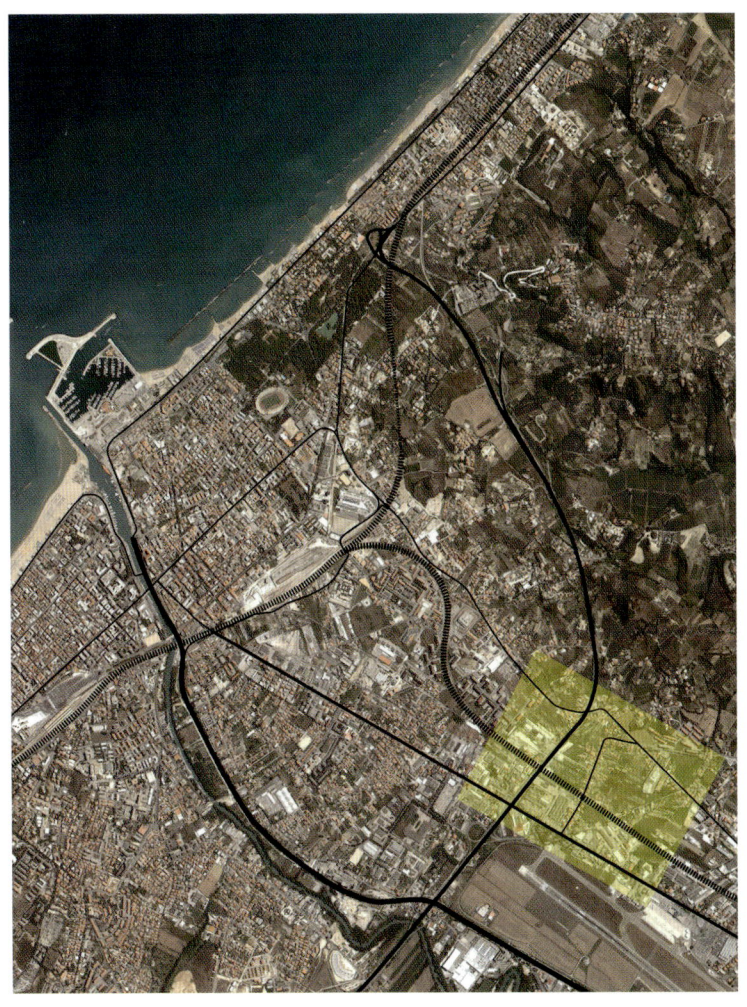

Pescara - Fontanelle areas and urban context

Pescara, Fontanelle areas, urban plan of public development- Pescara city, Consultant Ilvi Capanna, Carlo Pozzi, Mario Ciuffi

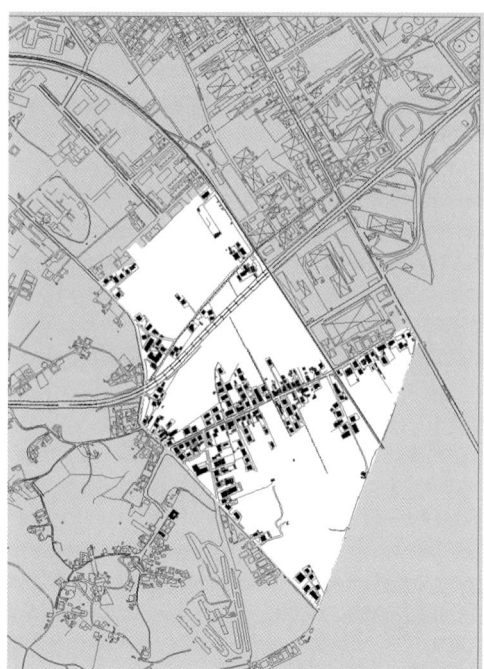

Pescara - Fontanelle areas, studies of urban plan

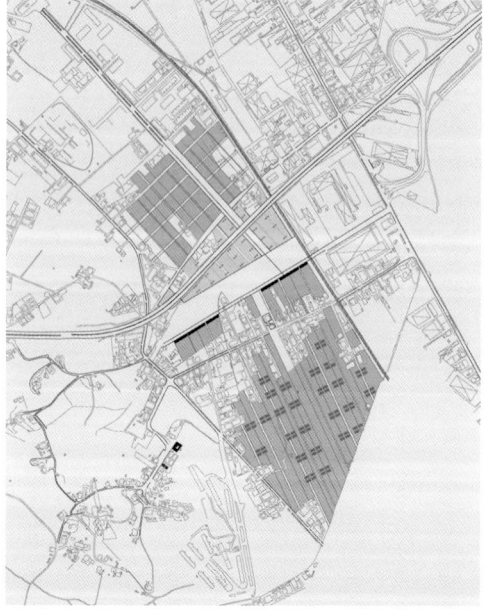

In particular, it is possible to recognize here how the relationship with the natural sites, open flat and hill areas has been almost completely bypassed in favour of a strict but morphologically weak urbanization, without supporting the complexity of the elements peculiar to its territory. The attention to the condition and the possible design solutions of the residential settlement area in suburban contexts requires two types of analysis. On the one hand, the consideration of the house analyzed in itself, as a building aimed at meeting the needs of the contemporary way of living; on the other hand the house considered as a fundamental part of the process of construction and transformation of city and territory. "The theme is not new, rather it stands out for its relevance, for the rapid movement and hybridization of people and cultures. The point is identifying significant examples of a building and typological tradition that combine the recognition of urban layouts with the quality of *being inside* the house"[5]. The general point of view, referred to the city as a whole and in its complexity, and the particular point of view, referred to the "construction" of the single-family house and the way in which these houses can be grouped, can coexist in a research aimed at identifying the most important elements of the contemporary living.

The present city can certainly be understood as a crossable organism, in which "flows and fluidization processes of space" are supported, away from incisive separations and unnecessary limits. The contemporary residential systems, particularly in suburban-extended contexts, may arise as integrated, crossable fields, in a continuum with the whole urban area, but at the same time as fields with a certain degree of autonomy, formal recognition, predetermined separation from important traffic flows. So "individual attitudes and conditions of freedom of the whole urban system" combine in these fields.

With reference to residential areas, as V. Gregotti states, it is essential to reverse the principle of independent residential district, heir of the egalitarian tradition of the Modern Movement. It is also necessary to define not opposition but dialectic between the overall network and the local identity, "which gives an important role to slowness and stratification and has to consider as essential material of the architecture project not only the built space, but also the relationship between the built space and the project space of the ground as a common ground". According to this hypothesis, such relationship must become the morphological basis of urban renewal[6]. It seems correct in this sense the use of less urban geometries, capable of including building fabrics and nature, a coexistence of city and nature that confer recognition and meaning to a fragmented and dispersed context as the suburban one. Cino Zucchi defines them as porous territories, "where parts of nature as fractals creep into the urban continuum, where the boundaries between city and landscape have become undefined"[7], recovering or reinventing significant spatial relationships. They are ways of definition and re-qualification peculiar to the contemporary lifestyle, where the needs of individual identification in the place of residence co-exist with the awareness and real condition of belonging to an overall fluid and crossable urban system.

The detailed plan of the Fontanelle area[8], referred to the Pescara western suburbs, taken as a reference point in the teaching experience of the Composition 2 courses[9], foreshadows a defined and articulated morphologically urban section integrated within the continuity of the area. In this part, the system of open and public spaces and relationships with the city is considered as a fundamental structural condition.[10] In the plan there is the ambition towards continuity with the urban context, but at the same time it is also possible to identify a need for autonomy, recognition, identification with specific places in the urban area covered by the project. This refers to the idea of a city defined by residential open blocks marked by significant separations from the most problematic areas of the territory. It is explicit the idea of assembling a part of the "city effect" through a variety of residential choices, services and facilities included in the urban continuum.[11]

The design of the residential area consisting of single-family detached or combined units is analyzed in the teaching experience of the Composition 2 course, taking into account both the actual meaning of the detached house and the relationship between this and the place it belongs to. It is a place-settlement area included and interrelated to the complexity of the various urban parts, but with a definite, independent identity. In the project of the students the problems related to the building sector (use of the plot, types, building systems, distributive aspects of the house) intertwine with those relating to the definition of blocks and public free spaces of contextual reference. The design of a four-family residential building with attached garden areas represents a fundamental part of didactic work. The building, consisting of four units, is interpreted primarily from the point of view of morphology, as a constitutive element of the residential area defined by detached houses, a part of the overall detailed plan. The constraints arising from the unification of the individual units with two blind walls lead to an analytical study of the plans of the two levels. They have to be defined considering the relationship between the interior space of the house and the outdoor garden space as a basic element of the project. In addition to the four-family building, the plan provides for two grouped dwelling units or

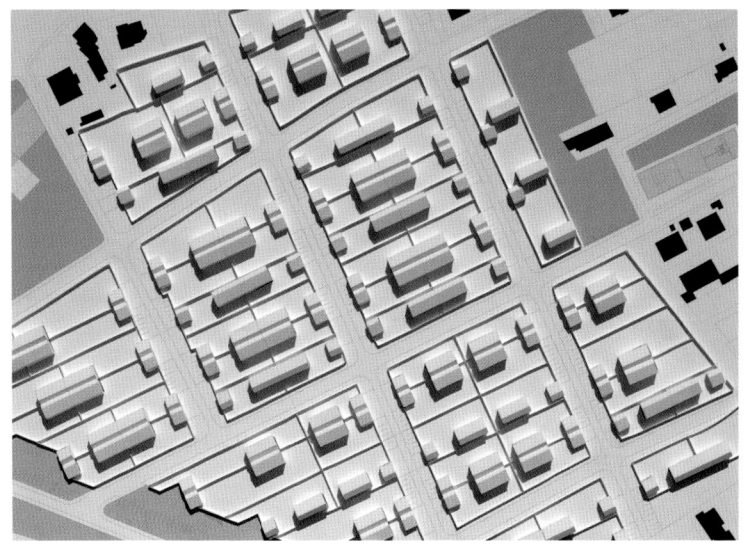

Single-family homes – study
Students A.Acciarri, F.Andreozzi, B.Buttazzo, M.Chimienti

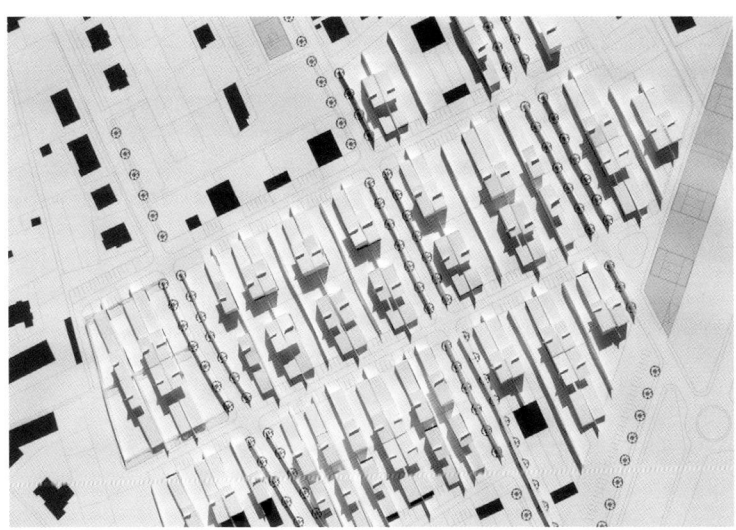

Single-family homes – study
Students L. Magagnano, R. di Lorio

Students A.Acciarri,
F.Andreozzi, B.Buttazzo,
M.Chimienti

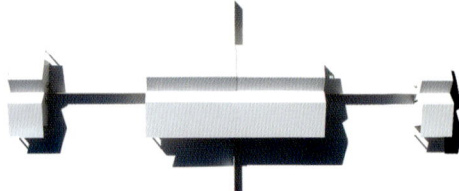

Students F.Brozzetti,
D.Castellano, C.Cervi

Students D.Chiavarini, S.Toso

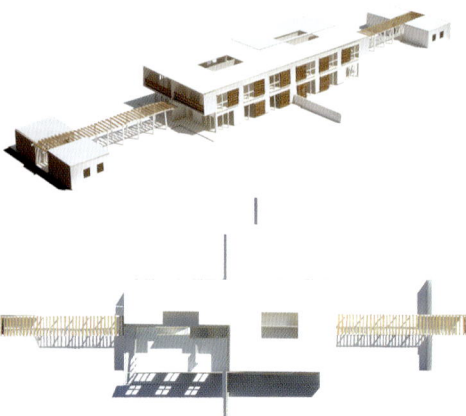

independent detached units. In the many cases elaborated, this results in drawings of open blocks in which the parameter of variability, mandatory condition intended as a response to contemporary living needs, is subjected to a formal overall principle. The dwelling units are therefore designed through distributive solutions including the possibility of variations in the articulation of the plans and in the design of elevations.

In the teaching experience, along with the study of modern and contemporary fundamental experiences related to the detached house type, reading the existing condition of the areas covered by the detailed plan is an essential part of the students' work.[12] The settlement composed of detached houses is designed from the XIX century to the present through a variety of possible type-morphological configurations representing a laboratory of continuous experiments for architects.[13] The design of the detached house and the way houses are grouped occurs in the laboratory within a defined path of historical and current knowledge and through the investigation of the multiplicity of contextual relationships and significant references to contemporary urban and architectural strategies. The most significant contemporary experiences related to suburban low-density residential areas investigate the historical and identity value of the detached house in its many variants combining it with the role played within the extended urbanized area, similar to that of a great city "in which more or less dense areas, central and suburban places, urban and territorial suburbs functionally integrate"[14]. In the event of settlement hypotheses subjected to the essential architecture and urban checks we referred to, the design of the detached house becomes part of the conscious construction of the contemporary city.

NOTES

1. "The urban fabric has frayed; consequently, the city has assumSed an unprecedented identity. The suburbs become the dominant feature, too wide and never fully programmed, characterized by significant social differences with situations with severe deficits in communication and services. Therefore, the city loses its traditional appearance and its nature. It breaks losing that part of a continuum peculiar to its various elements and the urban fabric expands and opens with no apparent structure". Paolo La Greca *"le periferie nella città contemporanea: caratteri e strategie per il recupero", in: Modelli di sviluppo di aree urbane di piccole dimensioni – a cura di Mauro Francini, Franco Angeli ed. 2009.*

2. "The concrete frame silently invading the territory and marking the end of the division between city and countryside can be considered an expression of the geographical epoch-making transformation that nowadays, in different contexts, seems to spread pervasively and unimpeded. The cities - which in the collective imagination are still those of a century ago - responding to the title of "historic centres" are actually agglomerations without boundaries nor hierarchies. Elvira Petroncelli: "Traiettorie di sviluppo urbano", in: *Modelli di sviluppo di aree urbane di piccole dimensioni – a cura di Mauro Francini, Franco Angeli ed. 2009.*

3. The expansion based on "periurban fringes" produces a chaotic and fragmented settlement fabric, which tends to incorporate larger and larger portions of territory. "The city of the urban fringes is a cruel devourer of landscape. It extends its fractals in every direction. It does not stop even in front of the monuments of history embedded in the rural landscape. Only shreds will remain of the ancient villas, with their estates and gardens. They will be surrounded by the ugly residential, commercial and industrial plots of the suburbs". Carlo Socco, Andrea Cavaliere, Il bordo della città – OCS Osservatorio Città Sostenibili, Dipartimento Interateneo Territorio – Politecnico e Università di Torino – Working paper P09/07.

4. V. Gregotti, "Elementi di disegno urbano ordinati secondo i principi della modificazione urbana" – Casabella 588 marzo 1992.

5. AA. La casa, Forme e ragioni dell'abitare, (a cura di Luciano Semerani) Skira 2008.

6. V. Gregotti, L'architettura nell'epoca dell'incessante, Editori Laterza 2006.

7. Cino Zucchi, "Un nuovo disegno urbano", su: Lotus 120 – Urban housing (2004).

8. Project for a detailed plan for the Fontanelle area in Pescara - Public plan, Pescara municipality – Consultants: Ilvi Capanna, Carlo Pozzi, Mario Ciuffi.

9. Courses of Architectural Composition 2, R. Branciaroli, I. Capanna School year 2008-2009. Students taking part to the workshop use the detailed plan for the Fontanelle area as a reference, analyzing it as a whole and applying it in particular to the development of the single-family residential area arranged in the plan.

10. Pierluigi Nicolin, Elementi di architettura, Skira 1999 pag.64** "Bernardo Secchi, city planner and theorist, believes suburbs is an inappropriate term to represent something that avoids any definition. He notes that the suburbs are not only the place of subordinate activities, of degradation. The suburbs are also the margin, the exchange zone between city and territory. The organic representation of the city is a wrong picture to understand the reality of the suburbs and metropolis of our time. It is incompatible with the emergence of a vast and coherent set of differences in the modern society".

11. The adoption of the strategy based on the diversification of the constituent elements is a central part of the Fontanelle detailed plan. The strategy is

conceived as a possibility of combination able to facilitate the efficient mixing of building types, high-rise multi-family buildings, single-family detached buildings, spaces and community services.

12. The current existence of diverse and multiple cultural positions introduces the need, especially from an educational point of view, of a careful selection of experiences, focusing in particular on those in which the shapes of architecture more clearly express the intrinsic and essential reasons of living, those in which the identity issues inseparable from the theme itself are explicit.

13. The search for alternative settlement solutions to the traditional city characterizes all the nineteenth century, becoming specific in the Modern Movement with typological solutions that starting from the study of the individual houses result in a variety of housing grouping types. The debate includes a reflection on the diverse cultural currents at the base of the modern project, on the multiple interpretations regarding the intrinsic meaning of the house. According to some authors, it is a place of essential identity, a living space in continuity with the past shapes; according to others, it is a standardizable, repeatable, combinable element based on defined and specific types, with endless configurative solutions. Here we refer particularly to the advanced stage of the Modern Movement (Frankfurt Congresses, 1929 and Brussels, 1930) which gives priority attention to the "housing" rather than the "house", determining in many cases a strict typological approach, with the provision of quantitative generalizable standards.

14. Cesare Macchi Cassia, Il grande progetto urbano - La forma della città e i desideri dei cittadini, La Nuova Italia Scientifica, 1992.

6

A plan for Fontanelle

Carlo Pozzi

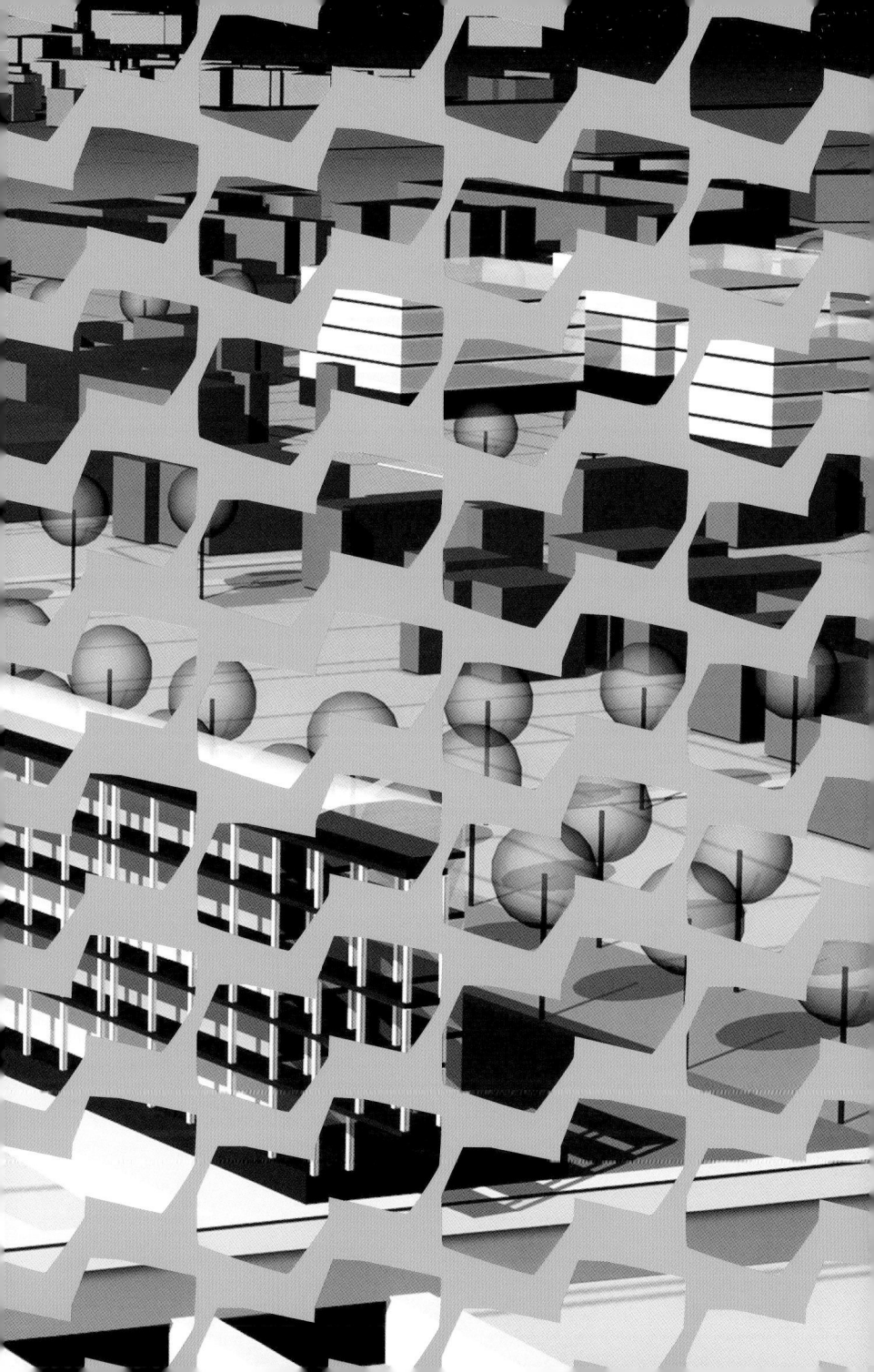

Draft plan, compared with the existing

Foreword

The process of expansion of the city seems to incessantly proceed without proper reflection. But just where the settlement areas freely and randomly connect, resulting in the phenomenon of urban sprawl - in this case we refer to the mid-Adriatic coastal city - within urban development there still are encysted rural areas that can play an important role as a link between city and countryside, sometimes reducing the overall urban impact.

When formulating the first post-war reconstruction plan of Pescara, Piccinato was thinking of a process of inner densification of housing types that would diminish and dilute towards the coast, alluding to the vocation of *garden city* proposed by the city of the first years of the twentieth century. We worked as consultants of the Department of Urban Planning of the municipality in formulating the first proposals of the detailed plan for Fontanelle, between Pescara and Sambuceto. Then, we followed a similar procedure, confirming the role of urban density acquired by the areas adjacent to the working-class neighbourhoods of a few decades ago, and reducing it to the edge of town with the proposal of a garden city consisting of single-family houses. They make reference to and strengthen an already existing trend, recording and interpreting it within a new quality of urban design, road layouts, green areas.

Fontanelle today

The plan covers a flat area alternating and overlapping rural fragments with urban peripheral elements. The Fontanelle valley area, between Tirino Street and the railway, from Aldo Moro district to the north up to the boundary with Sambuceto to the south, with a southern part reaching Tiburtina Street, is predominantly empty with only one recognizable urban element, namely, Fontanelle Street. In a general state of decay and neglect, we can distinguish some specific urban problems:

1. Lack of cross-sectional roads compared to the Pescara valley area: the only one existing, Fontanelle Street, is wholly inadequate to ensure the crucial relationships between the foot of the hill, Tirino Street, and the centre of the valley, Tiburtina Street;

2. The motorway viaduct, based on pillars, splits the area of the plan into two non-communicating sections, because of the inaccurate use of the underlying spaces (generally deposits and fenced lorry parks);

3. There are four high-tension power lines and related pylons in the area. Three of them, from the railway to Tirino Street, run through the

north part of the area up to the boundaries with Aldo Moro district. The fourth, instead, involves the whole area, from north to south, also flying over residential areas and a school.

The cumbersome presence of infrastructures

First and foremost, the project aims at interpreting the infrastructure interruption by constructing topographic and building lines crossing it, while maintaining the necessary distances by law, also thanks to the proposal of de-spading the power line to serve the railway facilities. Today the power line crosses the residential area (including a school) without complying with the minimum distances provided for by the laws in force.

A public park will be built on the edge of the existing district and it will become an element of relationship between old and new established communities. A section of the park will be devoted to community gardens also related to a broader area, accepting from a planning point of view the indication of use already present in the area and peculiar to many edge areas in European cities.

Regarding the new traffic regulations, the ones belonging to the planning instrument in force are adopted and interpreted, giving more value to a new street parallel to Fontanelle Street and suggesting a relationship between the two also with reference to the direction of traffic.

Aldo Moro Street extends towards Fontanelle and the airport, as a completion of the "green way" which in the PRG (General Zoning Plan) innervates the whole city, independently redefining, where possible, public transport and private vehicles routes, cycle tracks, pedestrian spaces.

Structure of the plan

It consists of four parts:
    a. *equipped green area*
    d. *core area*
    c. *small residential building settlement* (north residential area)
    d. *garden city* (south residential area)

a. The equipped green area is structured between Aldo Moro district and the new expansion covered by the plan. The choice is motivated by the opportunity to build an enjoyment and aggregation centre for both parts, the old and the new one, but also by the presence of high-tension power lines. Considered the high cost of their de-spading, placing the park in this space would allow to leave three of the four existing lines. The fourth, instead, has to be necessarily undergrounded. Besides passing over residential areas and even a school, with its related side pylon, it would prevent any new construction in about half of the whole area. In the part towards the railway, shielded by a sequence of small boxes, the equipped green area is structured on urban gardens, following vocations already existing in the plan and a trend that is giving very interesting results in many urban and metropolitan areas of the planet, with the direct involvement of citizens. A special regulation will be drawn up for the gardens management.

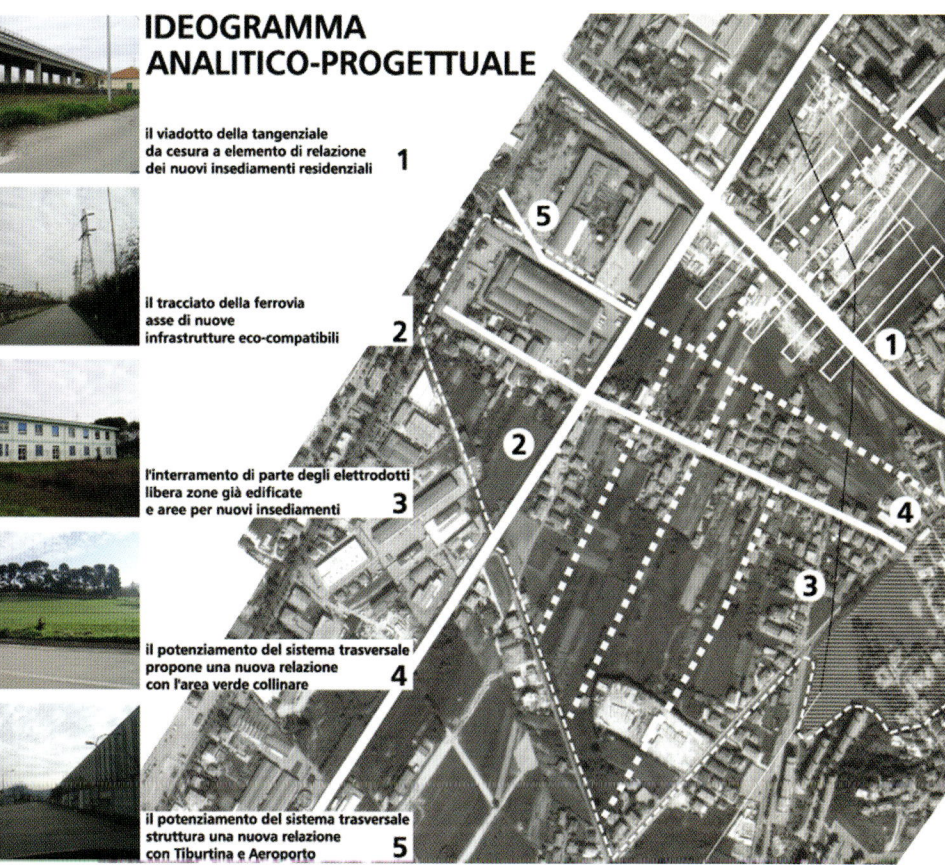

Table 1 Preliminary analysis

b. The core area, for its shape and location, meets three requirements:
- the construction of a cross architectural and urban area compared to the Pescara valley area (in this sense it does not replace the existing Fontanelle Street, but works with it, broadening the role of link and public space between Tirino Street and Tiburtina Street);
- the creation of an aggregation and reference centre for all the new urban extensions included in the plan (in fact, the residential area made of apartment blocks to the north and the completion of Fontanelle town mainly with single-family houses with garden to the south converge on it);
- the conclusion of the new central civil road, parallel to Tiburtina Street, namely the "green way" (with public buildings, businesses, mobility), from S. Donato district through Aldo Moro Avenue would reach the new Fontanelle settlement, forming the public spine of the whole urban valley area between Tiburtina Street and the south hills of Pescara city.

This new *urban centrality* is characterized by:
- an architectural backdrop consisting of residential buildings arranged in a row and linked by a portico, which will house commercial and public activities on the ground floor;
- a cycle-pedestrian area with the shape of an extended square;
- an equipped area with sports equipment, shielded by a sequence of service spaces, for dressing rooms, sports association premises, café.

The settlement, receiving multiple streams coming from the "green way" and connecting them to Tiburtina Street, allows a double type of one-way traffic, intense and multifaceted, for bicycles and cars towards Tirino Street (running parallel to Fontanelle Street, being one-way as well).

c. the small residential building settlement defines the northern residential area, joining the extension of Aldo Moro Avenue, defined in the PRG as "green way": a long road section to allow reserved lanes for public and private transport, a cycle track, pedestrian routes and areas, big trees and ground level car parks. The road system is completed with the links between Tirino Atreet and the completion of the road along the railway, and with other north-southward roads crossing the motorway viaduct up to the core area (b).

The apartment blocks are designed as residences. These are grouped into two or three on the basis of their location on a low basement (1,50 meters), matching with the elevation of the garden having the same height. This results in a urban block and therefore a "city effect", while maintaining its independence from the single units. In addition, the slight elevation, besides holding car parks and cellars in the basement, allows a good privacy of the ground floors, generally used as a residence, too, making it possible to allocate a part of the communal gardens to private gardens for the ground floors. The elevation of the communal green space allows the use "in situ" of the soil excavated for the foundations of the basement.

The area is crossed by the motorway viaduct. Although based on pillars, it represents a barrier because the underlying space is generally closed to public use. The plan proposes the liberation of that space from the existing activities, generally lorry parks, both because those activities are meaningless within the new urbanization and to allow vehicular and pedestrian links. In addition, this space could hold a significant spread out of the cycle track up to the Pescara river, future urban park, as well as a number of activities of public interest, sports and games.

d. The garden city defines the southern residential area and is a completion of the existing Fontanelle town.

There are four types of intervention:
- single-family houses with gardens are proposed for most part of the settlement;
- the built-up areas being now implemented are included in the plan;
- a sequence of small residential buildings with raised ground floor reaching Tiburtina Street is set up along the southern edge, bordering Sambuceto;
- a series of high-rise buildings arranged in a row close the settlement to the north and contribute to define the core area.

Single-family houses with gardens, with various grouping solutions, occupy almost the entire available surface. It is a type of detached house with box-garage outside the house. This choice allows to give a better shape to the free spaces pertaining to the single house, building a patio between it and the garage and a real garden. This green area, together with a system of tree-lined streets and cycle tracks, gives to the whole area the idea of a garden city.

Other interventions introduce some differences in the homogeneous structure of single-family houses, giving to that structure a greater architectural and urban importance and solving particular situations. Some built-up areas already present in the PRG are included within the intervention. If they are already in an advanced stage of definition, they are taken as such. For the others, whose planning parameters have already been defined, the plan proposes a provisional architectural definition and the creation of public gardens in these residential areas obtained through the connection of public green spaces belonging to those built-up areas with others included in the detailed plan.

A "urban door" will be built for the area facing Tirino Street, necessary to prevent a possible condition of isolation of the interior part of the residential area, through the construction of two commercial buildings with raised ground floors and a big garden, obtained through

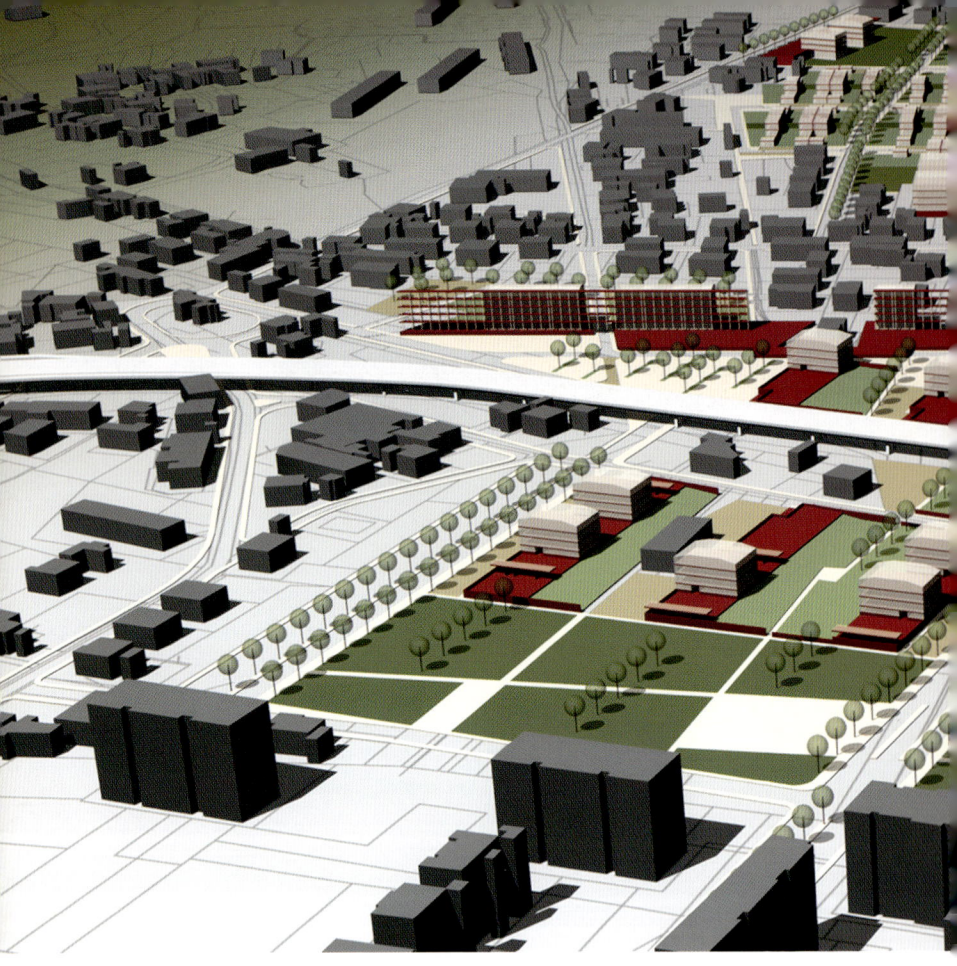

the connection of public green spaces belonging to the built-up areas with others included in the detailed plan. The southern edge, bordering Sambuceto, is also a variation in the residential structure. Here, another important cross-section road in relation to the valley area will be built with the construction of a new road with related railway flyover. The plan includes a big and varied public space extended from Tirino Street up to Tiburtina Street, consisting of ground level green spaces, car parks and basements of various heights, on which buildings similar to the north ones are set. However, they are defined to meet specific needs such as houses for special groups (the elders, young couples, the evicted) and characterized by commercial buildings towards Tiburtina Street side.

Dimensional view of the plan
Central system

Sustainability and urban environmental friendliness

The detailed plan wants to help promote culture, practice, quality of sustainable living, encouraging a *new quality of building* able to combine the themes of environmental sustainability and energy cost-savings with those of urban and architectural quality. The project proposes a range of solutions related to private building to be set up starting from these assumptions:

Carlo Pozzi

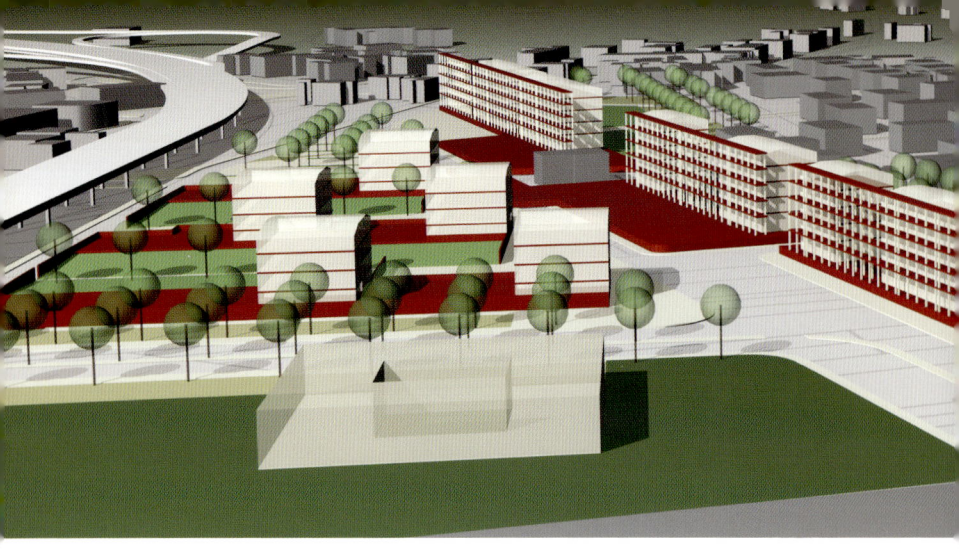

- *morphological and typological quality of the intervention*, in relation to the environmental, social and economic context;
- *energy and environmental quality*, focusing on energy cost-savings through the structuring of passive systems with natural cooling and preventing heat loss;
- *technological innovation* with affordable building and management costs, using eco-sustainable materials.

The plan also proposes a range of possible solutions to improve *the sustainability of the whole built-up* area subject to a new residential settlement:

- reduction of noise pollution thanks to noise-abating barriers with photovoltaic covering along the viaduct and the railway; implementation of a one-way traffic scheme to ease motor vehicle traffic; making the "green way" fully operational through public transport with dedicated track; the integration with pedestrian routes and cycle tracks, facilitating movements for the disabled;
- ecological balance, ratio between built or paved surfaces and permeable surfaces, with the proper distribution of trees in particular along the roads: trees belonging to the rural tradition, hedges, shading vines;
- new forms of waste collection, with simple systems for differentiation and the introduction of composting to be managed mainly in the green area;
- a possible cogeneration plant with energy distribution produced by district heating and district cooling networks and the consequent reduction of climate-changing gas emissions.

Three-dimensional view of the plan
In the foreground the buildings, the viaduct over the arcaded buildings the central system and, ultimately, the garden city

* Professional advice has been provided by the architects Mario Ciuffi, Ilvi Capanna, Carlo Pozzi to the town Urban Planning Department: this text is a revised version of the programmatic statement approved by the Town Council in 2009.

7

Compression & dispersion

Ilvi Capanna

Country of Moscufo, foothills Abruzzo
Photo by Andrea Scorrano

When concluding my other article *Small and simple houses*, I made reference to two recent very different experiences: the Rudin house, whose abstract shape plays a role within the scattered alpine spreading, and Ypenburg houses linked instead to the planning tradition of the modern city, where the detached house faces the typical conditions of the city - repetition, grouping, uniformity and variation, etc. In this article, I will try to frame the meaning of shapes, the problem of their *necessity*, not so much according to a viewpoint basically focused on the building itself, but identifying that aspect within the broader discourse it participates in, in its overall constituent idea: detached house and settlement idea, from the most basic parcelling-out where the single-family house is detached compared to the plot (often a minimum one), and where the contrast between the origin of this type of house and the new state of urban compression is evident[1]. Or in more complex plans experimenting aggregative minimum standards, such as semi-detached or four-family houses, and where the elementary type of the house intersects other very different types such as the patio or the row. This is an aspect of the problem: the passage of the detached house from the countryside and nature to the city, from its condition of alternative to its increasingly massive use for the construction of the great modern city. This corresponds to the beginning of that general phenomenon that tends to deeply change the traditional structure of the territory, its articulation into specific shapes, clearly distinguished both for their internal features and for the sharpness of perimeters: city, countryside, nature.

In his *L'architettura della realtà (The architecture of reality)*, Antonio Monestiroli sums up this context, the inclusion of the single-family detached house among the elements of urban construction, distinguishing two important moments. The first one, during the XVIII century, represented by some American experiences, particularly the construction of Savannah city in Georgia, and by the physiocratic research in Europe. It is a trend of experiences that "radically critics the historical construction of the city, looking elsewhere, to the countryside, new principles of organization of life on the land", in particular Ledoux's ideal city, *the city surrounded by nature*. The other period is placed within the context of the nineteenth-century city where it "loses its meaning of alternative peculiar to the previous assumptions, and acquires the meaning of compensation to the rented house", where "... there are two different experiences: the workmen's house... the middle-class house"[2], and where the great theoretical effort of the garden city lies[3]. The process introducing the single-family detached house, until then intended as a representative element of the distinction between city and countryside, among the urban housing types, starts to develop. It is part of the more general process that will lead to the *open block*, to the crisis of the block itself within the urban growth, to the division of the elements of the compact city, and to the overlapping between city and countryside.

It is a period of great innovation not only in the evolution of the idea of city, but more generally of the idea of human settlement in the land, a precondition for a radical change of the age-old relationship between city and countryside. That little house surrounded by the rural world enters the urban context bringing its principle of dispersion, attempting to combine with the other opposite principle of compression peculiar to the city. This difficult and unsolved relationship between compression and dispersion, centrifugal force and centripetal force, from now on will mark the destiny of the city, to find itself unresolved in the context of widespread contemporary settlements[4].

Eberstadt already highlighted this unsolved problem stating that "the Groszstadt compared to the old city is characterized by the centrifugal force dominating its evolution, compared to the concentration force that produced the conditions for the definition of the ancient city"[5]. Later, Hilberseimer recognized the need to move forward in addressing the urban problem. "... The decentralization is a trend of our time, to a much greater extent than we are willing to admit. ... As soon as possible, due to the lack of planning, you will encounter the same chaotic situations in the countryside and the same poverty that prevail in our cities. This is already demonstrated by the suburbs that arise without limitations around our cities..."[6].

However, from now on, neighborhoods made up of small houses with their kitchen garden or large middle-class villas will be part of the urban landscape, among the possible choices in the city. Generally speaking, at least before the uncontrolled contemporary urban sprawl, they are built using simple parcelling-out plans setting shape and dimensions of streets and *blocks*, and their subdivision into plots centrally occupied by the detached house.

Regarding this aspect, the experience of workmen's villages is a model: *Nuova Schio* in Vicenza, *Crespi d'Adda* dating back to 1878 and preserved intact until today, *ville Menier* in Noisiel. In Pescara we find the Pineta district, in the southern part of the city, which was not really born as a workmen's village, but was actually built and inhabited only with the construction and development of the plant of Aurum factory. Through archive documents, Piero Ferretti traced the parallelism of plant, development and consolidation between the factory and the Pineta district, the south Pescara: it is a strong bond from the beginning, abruptly interrupted by the closure of the factory. "...The building is divided into 52 blocks (insulae) by perpendicular roads called longitudinal if parallel to the sea, and cross roads, if perpendicular to the first ones, with the exception of the only two inclined roads that form the so called trident starting from the Kursaal. The plots show an approximatively 800 to 1000 square meter extension. Nevertheless, the recurrent surface is a 840 square meter area: 28 meters is the size of the plot on the crossroads, given that the distance among the longitudinal roads is 56 meters and the plots are arranged in two rows; 30 meters is the width of the front on the longitudinal roads.

The parcelling-out starts 40 meters from the foreshore and, on the opposite side, there is the only road with a non-straight line bordering the pine forest. The distance from the boundaries is defined in relation to the plots location: 5 meters from the boundaries for the buildings on the first longitudinal road, hierarchically the most important, 2 meters in the other cases. In the rectangular blocks the building is expected to be aligned with the south side of the road line, and the

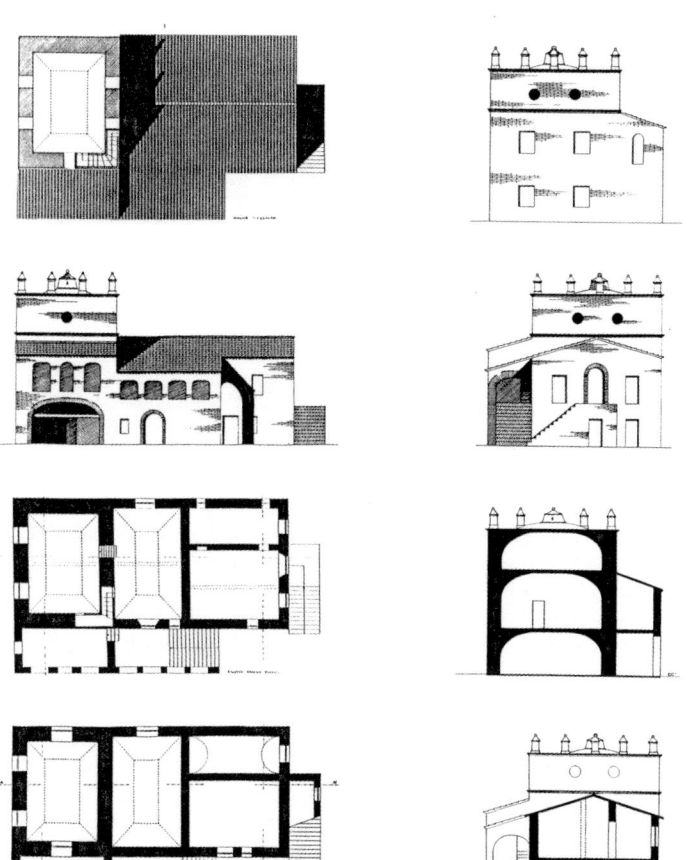

Farm of the tower, the town of Cellino Attanasio, Teramo

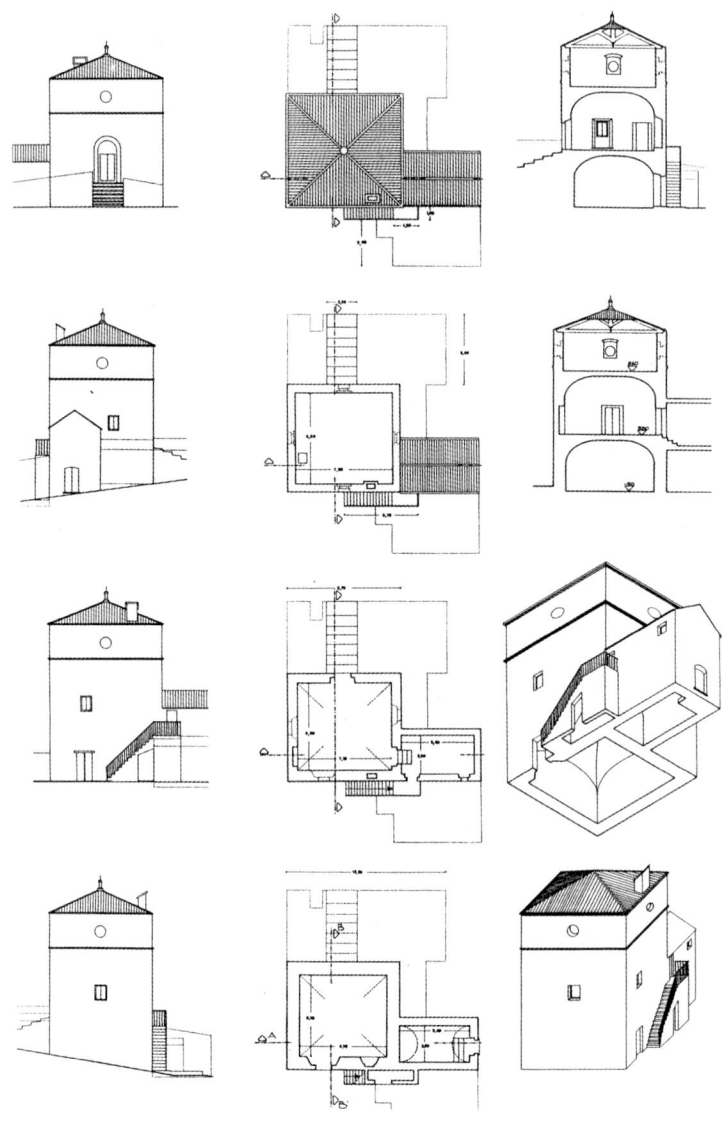

Tower House Fontecchio, province of Teramo

combination of plots for the construction of large villas is allowed"[7].

Probably the relationship with the pinewood and the sea, the true public spaces of a modern city as Pescara, and the consolidation of a collective sense of living through the development of the Aurum factory and its enlightened management[8], led to the success of this part of the city reaching us as one of the most livable residential areas, although much altered.

Generally speaking, in these experiences we can see a kind of elementary urban shape, almost a resetting of historical experience, a return to the camp or village. Yet it now constitutes a large part of the world urban settlement, albeit with very different variations, from the chaotic and increasingly unlivable urban sprawl, such as the Italian experience, to the North European or North American experiences where it is evident the search for possible conjugations, for integrative weak systems internal to this housing choice, and at times for possible integrations with *natural* elements, such as forests, rivers, reserves, etc. What is certain is that at the beginning of its urban history the detached house criticized the compact city in front of its nineteenth-century growth, and thus brought with it the dissolution of the block and the tendency to form related residential units but isolated in nature and in the countryside. The current scenario shows us endless urban extensions, which tend to identify with the macro-elements of geography, valleys, shorelines and coasts, more and more devoid of natural or rural discontinuities, and where, paradoxically, in the best of cases, the block is still the most commonly used. The thorough use of this housing type in the current conurbations worsened the problems the nineteenth-century city already showed, or more generally the problems of human settlements in the land, to the extent that some people hope, not without reason, a return to the compact block. The modern research from the theory of the garden city to Hilberseimer's studies, despite their clear and timely foresight, does not substantially affect the real condition except in very rare cases. The problem already highlighted by Eberstadt and Hilberseimer is increasingly critical in the contemporary settlement. In Abruzzo, for example, the section of the Adriatic conurbation between Pescara and Montesilvano can be defined with two pairs of faces. On the one hand, the sense of belonging, an exasperated localism as emancipation from any precise cultural identity; on the other hand, the generalizing tension of non-places[9] . On the one hand, the proliferation of differences irreducible to any formal structure; on the other, the strength of a totalizing scheme. The evidence of the linear agglomeration on the Adriatic railway-seaside trunk can hide the true complexity of this context. It is much deeper than it seems: it also includes the Adriatic by-pass, the motorway and the railway, and a number of road junctions crosswise moving inward. It is a scheme also made of large voids and a double orientation. This duality would correspond to two strongly opposed principles: linear conurbation and urban sprawl, compression and dispersion. Is it convenient reading this reality according to dialectics and the degree of expressive completeness of these two principles? They also seem to act within the same linear Adriatic agglomeration, which can be described as the process of linear compression of full elements of the city that never gets over a sort of space of resistance, the minimum plot area that not only the apartment blocks but even the churches tend to maintain and fence in. The sum of the elements does not produce anything but the sum itself, even when the compression gets to physically touch the elements[10].

The first parcellings-out usually hid the complexity of the problem under their apparent simplicity. Some studies and modern experiences seem to deal with it trying to find *weak* grouping forces, internal to the detached block type, but being the simple combination of multiple single-family houses to form larger blocks: for example, Giovannoni's studies for "small houses and cottages" of 1910, or the workmen's city by Menier in Noisiel, or the four-family houses by Wright for Cloverleaf. In these examples, which follow and develop the tradition of the semi-detached house, the basic idea of the detached block is kept in an increased volume through the combination of two or four units, where the single-family house gives up the *freedom* of all its fronts but gains a greater distance from the houses belonging to the contiguous plots. The free spaces can find a suitable shape and their own meaning within the urban context, not simply and totally the negative aspect of full spaces, as in simpler parcellings-out.

However, these experiences do not affect the basic contradiction. I made reference to the Pineta district of Pescara also because there is a detached house in it, built by Ermanno Flacco e Rosella Lorito, in whose lines we can just read this contradiction, the difficult relationship between detached house and city. After some time, this small house is consistent with the construction of a urban section and confirms the meaning against the many formalistic and speculative injustices suffered by the district, one of the very few contemporary interventions that correctly interpret the history and typology of the Pineta district. Moreover, it also can be placed together with that group of recent experiences compared to the ancestral image of the house, even though to some extent it differs from most of them because of its connection with

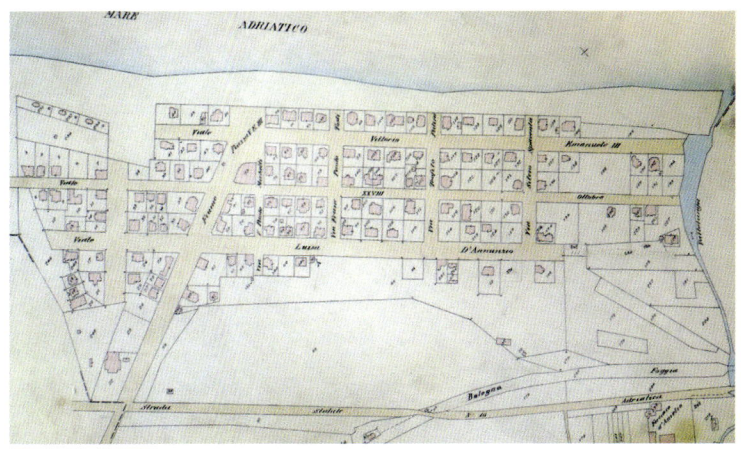

Pescara Pineta district, cadastral plan 1937
From: Piero Ferretti Aurum e Pescara sud, una costruzione in parallelo in: I. Capanna G. Tavano La fabbrica dell'Aurum in Pescara Carsa 2007.

Urban area in Maine, USA

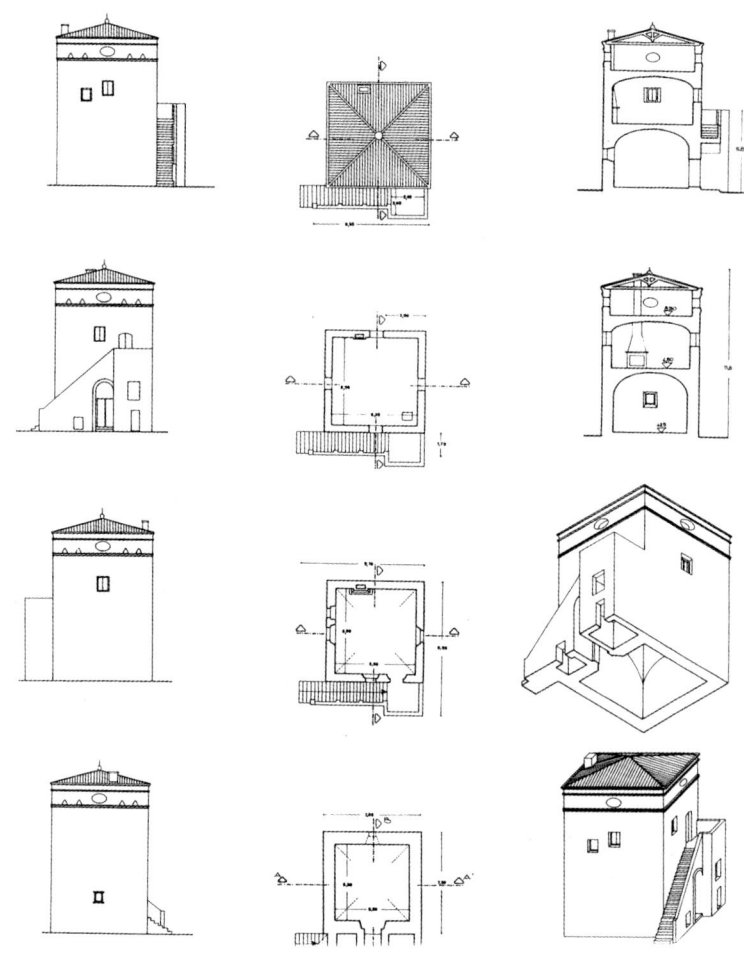

Tower House Fontecchio, province of Teramo

Lorito House, Pescara, Arch. Ermano Flacco, Rosella Lorito

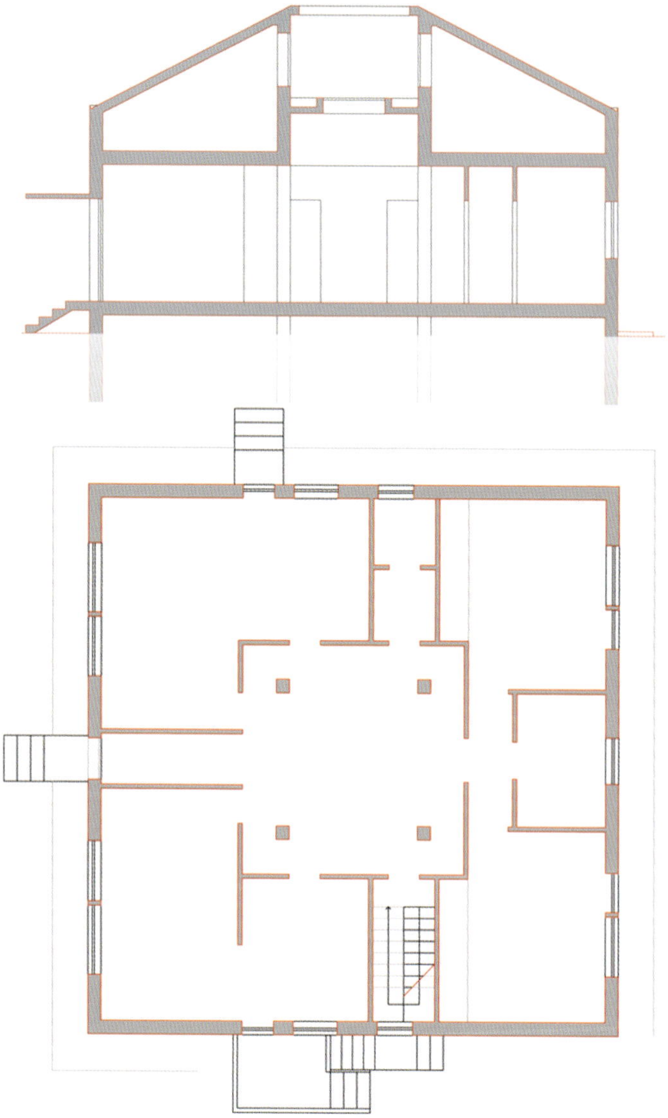

House Lorito, section and plan - material provided by the designer

the historical experience of the house. Here the house arises from a planning process which is also analysis, development of the theme in terms of time and within the urban context including it. So its interest in this discourse also involves the broader aspects of urban morphology. The architecture of its distribution system can be described as axial correspondence of the road level door and the house door ending in the small interior entrance hall, defined by four pillars and a translucent covering. The hall organizes the ground floor and discovers the vertical unit of the detached single-family house. The contradiction we see on the ground floor between the centralization of the hall and the house facing the surrounding garden becomes the specific characteristic of the house on the upper floor, with the bedrooms, where the introversion of its shape is absolute. In this way we also discover that the architecture of the roof is separated from any nostalgia for ancestral shapes, to tend instead to a status of necessary shape.

So its architecture clearly expresses that very difficult situation of compression/dispersion which accompanies the detached house in the city, through the typological intersection of two basic opposite principles: the block facing the outside space and the courtyard facing the inside space. It tells us what the original neighborhood and its houses were hiding under their apparent simplicity: building the big city or endless conurbations with detached houses is not a matter of little importance. It also implies a moving forward in typological research, a further refinement of that type of house that accompanies the human story from the beginning.

On the other hand, the very typological intersections are the basis of some contemporary experiences that attempt to combine dispersion and compression in their strategies of urban system. Regarding this aspect, it is very clear the residential unit designed by MVRDV studio for the island of Hagen in Ypenburg. The process of the project clearly emerges from the zenith sight. The installation of the four sections that make up the residential unit shows a kind of sliding correspondence between the different detached blocks, which seems to allude to the initial moment of the design process, where each of the four sections would be resolved with a single continuous line of row houses with the ridge parallel to the road. The second part of this hypothotical procedure sections the continuity of the row and shifts the obtained different-sized single blocks. In this way, the morphology of the unit is specified in relation to the relationship between two very different basic housing types: the side attached block and the detached block. However, this relationship keeps evident the two opposing principles we can even read in individual buildings, in the many blind walls or in the distributive solutions. The overall objective of this type of experience can be defined as identification within the architectural instruments of weak grouping forces for the detached house, as possibility to translate this into the urban context, from the freedom of the countryside to the urban compression. This objective is also included in the detailed plan of Fontanelle in Pescara[11], particularly in the south area arising as the completion of the old village of Fontanelle. It is evident the unfinished process of construction of this village in the zenith view: a first alignment of detached houses along the road and then the usual system of depth diagonal growth compared to it. It is particular in this case the evidence of the relationship between this system and the design of plots, visible even in what remains of the narrow extended fields, despite a typological choice: the detached house with surrounding garden, very different from the row. The project for the area includes the essential features of this ancient network of fields in order to achieve the greatest possible integration with the existing village, to form together with this a single residential unit between Tirino Street and the railroad with its underground station.

Starting from this old rural network the plan sets out a grid system, on which single-family houses grouped together are placed in different ways: two, four or single-family houses. So it is possible to vary the volume of individual blocks, both in size and shape, from the closest to the square to the most extended, without compromising the order of the grid. The single plot is divided according to a constant scheme - two-floor dwelling, guest house, stone pavement and garden - which allows a certain freedom of movement along the north-south axis of the grid. On the east-west axis, instead, the arrangement of the elements and the alternation of full and void spaces follows the short section of the grid. This system aims at achieving the general objective defined above by means of two elements.

One is compared to the chaotic process of overlapping and mutual fragmentation between city and countryside, which in general distinguishes the contemporary settlement phenomenon[12]. The plan tends to organize the private free space alternating built-up areas with free areas. The latter are formed by the uninterrupted succession of private gardens, approximately reflecting the extended shape of the old rural fields with a narrow front facing the new streets. The parcelling-out of plots allows to form continuous spaces with these gardens, without buildings, crossing the whole area and cut only by the streets. These spaces keep and bring into the city the dimensional width and a sense

From the work of students Cifolelli Elena, Chiara Corsi, Anna Cutrino, Course of architectural composition, prof. I. Capanna

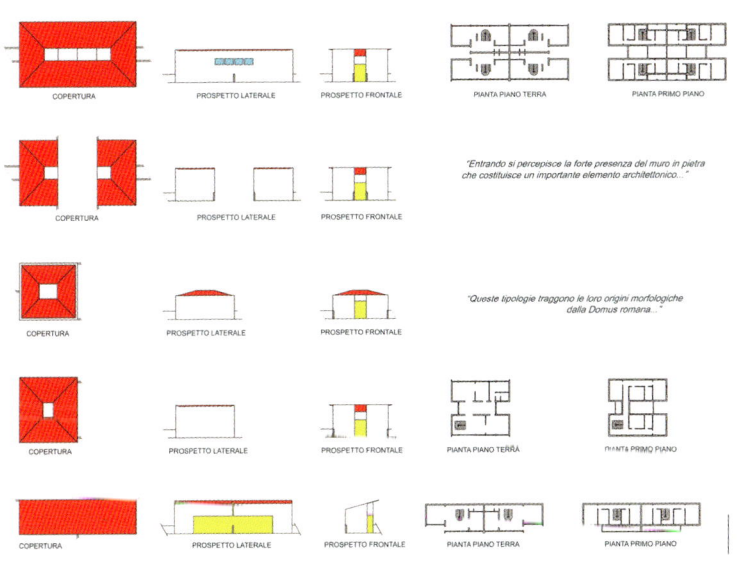

Course of architectural composition - students Simona Rinaldi, Michele Severini

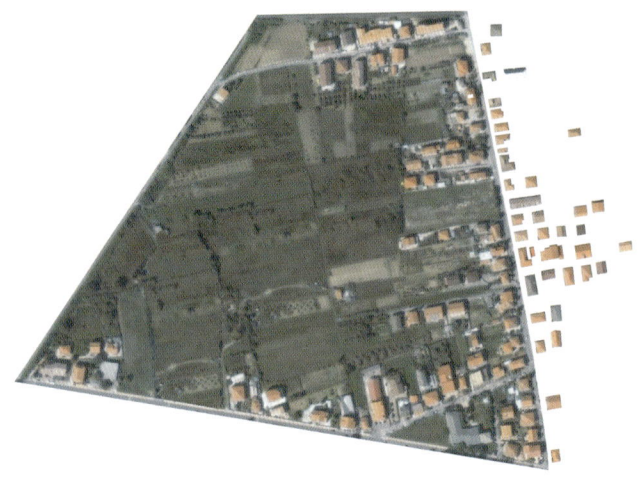

Homes low, of Fontanelle completed
by Piano Particolareggiato di Fontanelle in Pescara,
piano di iniziativa pubblica con la consulenza di:
I. Capanna, C. Pozzi, M. Ciuffi on a graphics processing

of freedom typical of the countryside. The other element addresses the condition of the detached house in the city trying to keep the idea of the detached block, but within a complex grouping framework, not simply limited to the juxtaposition of two or four residential units, but in particular intersecting the detached block with other different typological principles. Therefore, taking the old network of fields into account not only allows for greater integration with the existing village, but puts into the new urban organization the basic principle of the row, of the old narrow and extended fields on the short side of a road or on a irrigation canal. So the built-up spaces are organized according to the following sequence: entrance from the road, guest house, stone pavement, house. The stone pavement enclosed on three sides and open to the garden tends to take on the meaning of the patio, directing the undifferentiated circularity of the block.

NOTES

1. It is certainly a physical compression due to the limitation of individual plots and the proximity of individual houses and urban morphological elements. This also corresponds to a sort of expansion of the house linked to a settlement complexity, the urban one, different from the rural or natural one: "The house is no longer our single house, what matters is not its shape and size, but its proximity to the cathedral. More generally, the house is the place where we are, our relationship with the buildings of the institutions of the city where we live…" A. Monestiroli *La qualità del progetto di architettura: il progetto della casa*, In: L. Semerani (cura di) *La casa. Forme e ragioni dell'abitare* Milano 2008

2. A. Monestiroli *L'architettura della realtà* CLUP 1979

3. L. Hilberseimer *Groszstadt architektur* Stoccarda 1927

4. ".. The Adriatic Coast, Pescara valley, Po valley, etc., define a settlement scheme described as spontaneous overlapping of the city on the countryside. However, this does not eliminate the countryside, as on a programme schedule where a writing overlaps another one without prior cancellation. The remaining parts of city and countryside together, like fragments of a settlement scheme, feature coherent, partially active, interrupted elements of belonging. One can say that the background is abolished, and we get so many transparent layers that each one is, compared to the others, background and figure at the same time. So, the nature we can think about, which seems possible to live in, emerge through the splits in the network of city and countryside…" I. Capanna *Sovrapporre, voce del lessico*, in: *in.fra Manuale Forme insediative e infrastrutture*. Politecnico di Torino, dipartimento di Progettazione Architettonica Ricerca 40% Marsilio, Torino 2002.

5. G. Grassi *La costruzione logica della architettura* Marsilio 1967. In quoting Eberstadt's thought, the author also clarifies the relationship with rationalism: "… the problem of the architecture of the new city lies in its building scheme aiming at the concept of unity. That unity was lost among the new dimensional conditions due to the consequent technical inadequacy…"

6. L. Hilberseimer *Un'idea di piano* Marsilio 1967

7. Piero Ferretti *Aurum e*

Pescara sud, una costruzione in parallelo; in: I. Capanna G. Tavano *La fabbrica dell'Aurum in Pescara* Carsa 2007. The Kursaal, the Pescara-Penne railway and the Liberi plan of 1910 are the first actions through which Pescara takes possession of D'Avalos pine forest: it begins the transformation into urban element. The goal of the plan was to enhance the area as residential space and tourist resort. It included a pretty district made of small houses, private gardens, tree-lined avenues. It was a basic idea of the city, typical of modern parcellings-out. However, it promoted two important relationships on a urban scale: one between the pine forest and the sea through a system of green spaces (avenues and private gardens), the other one between the entire area and the city settled through the assumption of the existing Kursaal as the core point of the plan (from the consolidated Pescara, the current L. D'Annunzio Avenue reached the Kursaal and then the sea).

8. I. Capanna G. Tavano *La fabbrica dell'Aurum in Pescara* Carsa 2007. The area really started to be built and inhabited only with the construction of the Aurum Distilleries in the old Kursaal, in 1919, and with the following expansion carried out by Michelucci. The implementation of Liberi plan goes hand in hand with the success and growth of this factory. In the majority of cases conceived as a residence for workers and Aurum managers, the small houses included in the plan and their tree-lined avenues are gradually constructed until building a recognizable part of the city in the Pescara urban landscape.

We can imagine the crisis and the closure of Aurum Distilleries as a kind of *urban trauma*: the parallelism of plant development and consolidation between the factory and the Pineta district, a strong bond from the beginning, is brutally interrupted. If for many inhabitants of the district, who still *lived* on the Aurum, the divestment constituted a serious problem also from the economic point of view, we can still assume that the Pineta district at the time had already reached a certain degree of autonomy from the factory. Certainly many families had to leave the neighborhood, that underwent a process of partial abandonment and replacement of its inhabitants, but even so it maintained that collective identity built together with the factory. This aspect would endure partly also within the rapid process of development and acquisition of urban complex that the whole area would follow from then until the present day.

The Aurum hooters marked life in the district from the beginning, before the construction of the church with its bells. In fact, the harmony between the Distilleries and the city around was not only economic but, also thanks to the choices of the enlightened entrepreneur Amedeo Pomilio, it had encouraged the development of a true collective nature of urban construction, quite a singular aspect within the modern and contemporary city where the collective character of city and architecture tends to be lost. We could venture a limit case: the residents of the Pineta district could recognize themselves, represent their lives in the shapes and activities of the Aurum, like the ancients did with cathedrals or theaters.

9. G. Marramao *Appartenenza e atopicità* in PPC n°14, DAU facoltà di architettura, Pescara 1994.

10. ".... The general settlement phenomenon in the region, at least between the piedmont area and the coast, can be defined with two major systems. The large network, simple comb scheme with a long dorsal spine on the narrow coastal plain and lateral extensions along the deep valleys, reaching the Apennine passes. The urban sprawl is ordered by the infrastructure strength, absence of a previous settlement scheme, tension towards non-places, parts of a broader system. The small network is a complex scheme extended on the hills and piedmont area, cut by the lateral extension of the comb: a fragmented urban sprawl overlapping the previous old spatial structure, a tension towards a sense of belonging. A satellite view would show the two very different systems: a strong linear agglomeration against a complex urban sprawl without dominant shapes. However, this distinction is not so clear: the areas of the big network are not composed only of urban linear agglomerations, but also of junctions from which they branch off towards internal areas, often confusing themselves with the junctions of the small network, as well as of major infrastructures such as the by-pass (not urban, but Adriatic), the motorway and the new railway tracks (with related stations). These infrastructures represent the linear spaces of the big network but they are not linearly urban. In addition, from an economic and social point of view, the two systems are mutually necessary: one spreads thanks to the other. The introduction in the ancient Abruzzian "*city-countryside*" of new elements such as linear conurbations and their junctions produces a strong settlement tension towards the plural and multiform, where the traditional meanings of nature, city and countryside tend to merge and overlap. The new elements offer a highly innovative territorial framework, which, however, has not moved forward from the break and fragmentation of the previous one. Instead, on the one hand, they confirm the traditional absence of dominant urban aspects, and on the other hand they deny that absence standing as a great urban wall, a limit, a contemporary inside and outside space, giving up the potential richness of the play of relationships between small and large network, between local and global..." I. Capanna *Una spaziovia dell'Adriatico* In: R. Branciaroli, I. Capanna *Spazi liberi* Sala Editori 2005.

11. It is a public plan being edited. I took part in it as a consultant for the architectural structure together with Carlo Pozzi and Mario Ciuffi.

12. A phenomenon already at the centre of Hilberseimer's studies collected in *Un'idea di piano* Marsilio 1967: "... Cities should acquire a more rural meaning and villages a more urban meaning. The countryside must be integrated into the city and this must be a part of the countryside.... This view clearly shows how it is possible for the city becoming a part of the countryside with meadows, fields and forests. The countryside penetrates everywhere in the city and becomes a part of it."

8
Appartenances

Paola Branciaroli

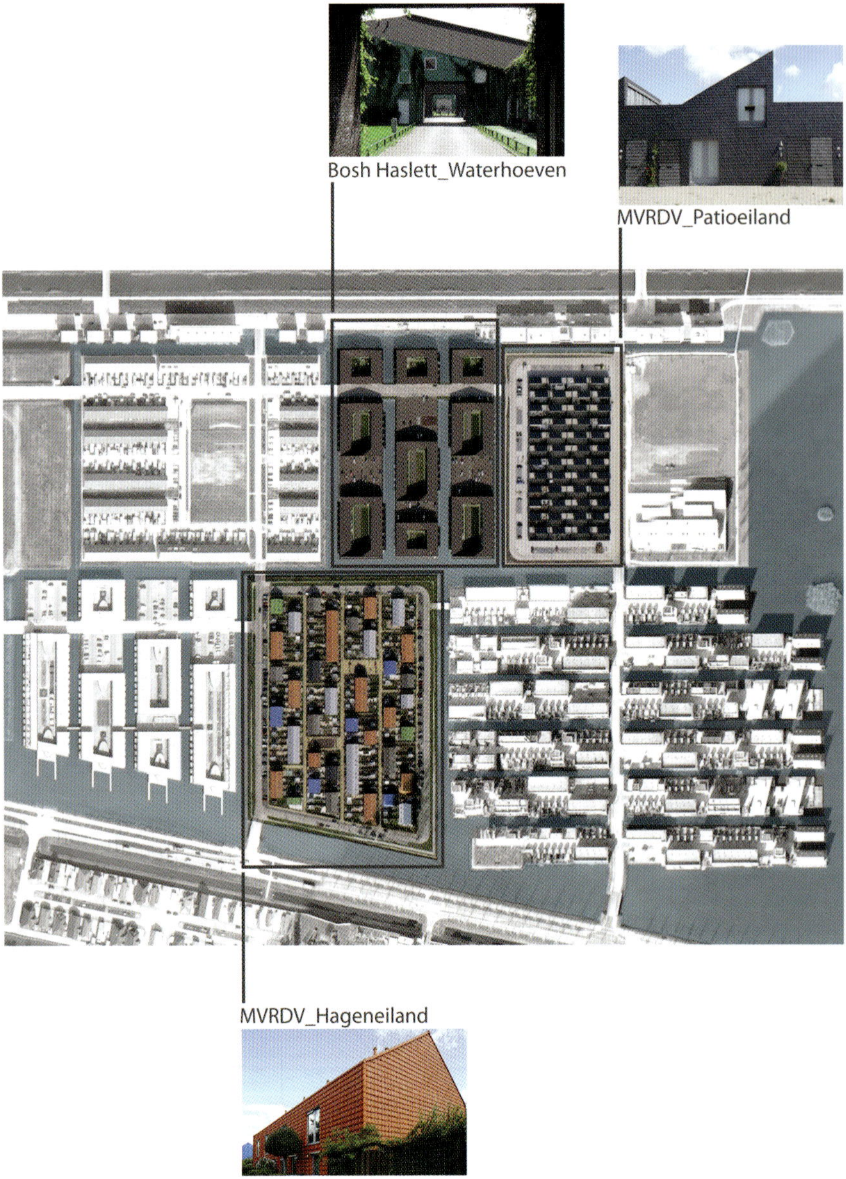

Bosh Haslett_Waterhoeven

MVRDV_Patioeiland

MVRDV_Hageneiland

MVRDV, Waterwijk, Ypenburg NL (1998-2005):
with identification of the three islands under study. Graphic reworking of Paola Branciaroli

Hageneiland is a urban island made up of detached houses with garden realised by the Dutch MVRDW group. It represents one of the new *socio-spatial models* the European architectural culture directs its attention to. It is properly one of the five islands included into the *Waterwijk Masterplan* developed between 1998 and 2005 by the same group of architects. It, in turn, is included within the Ypenburg *VINEX Plan* (*Vierde Nota ruimtelijke ordering Extra*) developed by *Friets Palboom* and *Els Bet* in 1994.

The Ypenburg VINEX Plan aims at converting by 2015 a big former military Dutch area into 11.000 housing units, commercial areas, public spaces and infrastructures so as to counter the shortage of lodgings and services caused by the increasing immigration, the reduction of families (more for the increased number of people living independently, rather than in large families) and the requests for individual space. Each of the five *theme districts (Waterwijk, Singels, Boswijk, Venen and De Bras)*, designed by different architects, shows a specific character and is in turn divided into smaller areas with a number of houses varying from 500 to 800 units.

In particular, *Waterwijk* holds a special position, because it presents itself as an archipelago of five groups of inhabited islands (850 houses in total) designed by three groups of architects and following as many *Concepts* resulting from a unique blend of cultures, religious beliefs, habits and lifestyles completely different among each other. These groups include *patio houses* (Patioeiland - MVRDW's project) and *detached houses with garden* (Hageneiland – MVRDW's project) that are going to be discussed below; *court houses* (Waterhoeven – Bosh Haslett's project), *apartments* and *reed houses* (Claus & Kaan's projects). Besides the typological differences, the above mentioned buildings can be distinguished by different green spaces, lighting systems, ecological measures and materials. All these interventions, so far from each other, are the result of a varied proposal meeting, on the one hand, the needs of a *composite society* and, on the other, re-evaluating the *individuality of each inhabitant*. Starting from the assumption that the *morphological configuration of a space* can surely facilitate the *meeting* and the *socialisation* of the inhabitants, it is worth noting how the different housing typologies create different *neighborhood relationships*.

Patio houses are completely closed to the outside space and they are separated both from the vehicular and pedestrian road network. The district is isolated from the surrounding area, as well as each person from the neighbours, enhancing the intimacy of the *family space*. Only the neighbours' barbecues remain in the foreground. A continuous wall sepa-

MVRDV, Patioeiland; wall continuous that separates the individual interior/exterior spaces from the private/public profound sidewalk of the
Photo by Paola Branciaroli

MVRDV, Patioeiland; the top openings overlooking on the large terraces the interior
Photo by Paola Branciaroli

rates the single *interior/private space* from the only *exterior/public space* represented by a deep sidewalk. The latter divides the apartment block from the car park, and therefore from the main road, allowing access to the *purely private space* of the house. The direct relationship between *private* and *public space* disappears, thus encouraging contemplative opportunities much more similar to oriental logics where perhaps only the wide terrace could become a public space of meeting (Fig. 2-3).

Unlike patio houses, the *court houses (Waterhoeven)* open around *common courtyards*. Due to their fundamental location and to their limited dimensions, these types of buildings take a *domestic nature* becoming almost extensions of the houses themselves. The main entrances of the houses give onto the *inner courtyards* without separating among them, to promote *socialising* opportunities. In continuity with the courtyards, more *public spaces* have been created: forecourts/parking spaces that can be used as play areas. In order to dismiss the very idea of limits and boundaries, *Waterhoeven big houses* have been placed on three longitudinal banks surrounded by canals creating a physical but not visual separation among them. At the same time, thanks to the balconies suspended over them, these canals encourage an *intriguing social life* also facilitated by the unique colour and the natural light of the court, the practice of gardening and the view one has from the accommodation. The terms *domestic space*[1], *urban space* and *nature* interfere with each other throughout the entire district. The *design* of this housing estate creates a *continuous non-hierarchical collective space*: the green area creeps into internal/public spaces while parking areas/forecourts acquire a domestic meaning.

In the case of *Waterhoeven* there is a new dimension of *collective co-existence* where the principle of "*My house is my neighborhood and my neighborhood is my house*" is in force. There can be identified close relationships of sociability and cooperation with neighbours so as to counter the isolation and marginalisation of individuals by stimulating a feeling of *belonging* both *to the community* and to the daily life places. In addition, *the welfare of the community* prevails on divergences and personal problems (Fig. 4-5).

Hageneiland, winner of the 2002 *Biennial Architecture Prize of the NAI (Netherlands Architecture Institute)* locates in between these two opposing conceptions of space and relationships of the dwelling. It is a neighbourhood of 119 low-cost houses for young families with children. These residences are the result/balance of the close economic ties of the period that guided the design in all its aspects (from the type of establishment to the constructive details).

Three methods have been used to meet the budget for its realisation. First and foremost, the vehicular infrastructure surrounding the entire plot and along which the only parking spaces were placed, has been minimized. Secondly, it has been decided to use a single coating material for each housing block. In order to ensure its recognition and diversification, five materials, each corresponding to various colours, have been chosen according to a series of tests on their level of healthiness and resistance to moulds: ceramic tiles, wooden tapered tiles, aluminum plates, fibro-cement siding corrugated panels and plates for the external finishing. Finally, the gutters have been removed: the architects themselves have properly called it *architecture without gutter because "the gutter is actually a strip of pebbles around the house"*. However, to

Bosh Haslett, Waterhoeven; he relationship with the channel creates physical separation but not visual trough the balconies suspended over, it intriguing that promote social life
Photo by Ilias Fragkakis

Bosh Haslett, Waterhoeven; the common court becomes the extension of the collective space constant, non-hierarchica
Photo by Ilias Fragkakis

obviate the lack of gutters, some small details, almost eyebrows, have been incorporated. These elements prevent the entry of rain from the windows becoming almost sculptural.

This has generated a series of houses with a strong *archetypal* and symbolic aspect: a simple volume with mansard roof and consequent *de-contextualisation* of the material that from covering becomes wall. It has to be considered a sort of ironic answer to the Dutch houses and the *concretization* of a *house scheme* idealised by the childhood imagination and represented in the *Monopoly* parlour game. To break the monotony of the neighbouring developments that built long rows of identical houses, ranging from twelve to twenty prefabricated units, and to increase the *social* and *typological diversification*, they have been cut and divided. In fact, the individual units, with the same dimensions but grouped in rows of two, three, four or eight, have been placed according to various combinations (in the front, middle or end part) within the private plot. This solution has created a wide *variety of crossed views*. By enhancing the perception of space, they increase the *open areas* and *social opportunities* for communication and allow to overcome any feeling of tightness in a very compact area (Fig. 6).

The *district* is based on a dense pedestrian network: five north-south routes cut the trapezoidal area of the plot into four long strips of ground and short distances cross them in a perpendicular direction forming a road neat and continuous space. It allows access to the various housing units by defining the *public space* consisting of two equipped green areas for children plays.

The *private garden*, typical of each house, becomes a *meeting place* rather than a filter between the inner and the outer space. The different position it holds with reference to the various houses (on the front, rear or both sides) creates different types of *visual relationships* (garden-garden, garden-house). In this way, the *meeting opportunities* are implemented, not only with the neighbours, but also with the neighborhood itself. These are facilitated by the practice of *gardening*, very popular in the Dutch culture. The willingness to avoid a clear separation between private and public space is also evident in the choice of the hedge as a material for shielding (not closing) a garden from the others. This specific element is what gives the name and character to the entire block. Within the garden of each residential unit there is a *warehouse/greenhouse*, namely a miniature house with a very elementary structure that can be dismantled, transported and built with different materials (wood, brick and glass). It becomes also an amplification disjointed from the house and a reversible tool to fill up interstitial voids. In this ornamental

MVRDV, the block; Hageneiland urban block shielded from the urban space through the hedge continues - Photo by Paola Branciaroli

MVRDV, Hageneiland; the public space consists of a green area equipped for children's play
Photo by Ilias Fragkakis

or vegetable garden every one can create his/her own green room and experience a personal *relationship with nature* (Fig. 8).

The range of these *spatial solutions*, within the binding starting grid, represents the emblem of the *freedom* of living in a flat area without strong points of reference. It proves that people are able to create a *complex* and variously modulated *community* even with simple and elementary building blocks. The *void space*, conceived as a connection between the houses and the *urban space*, dominates in the design and structures the relationship among people. On the contrary, the house arises from the need to group the elements around a *relational social space* that is *public*, *semi-private* or *private* at the same time. The buildings are not divided by spine walls anymore, but rather these spaces, as active mechanisms, unify and create *new relationships*, not only in a *physical* and spatial way, but also in a *social* one. As a matter of fact, when linking the different parts of the block, the *collective network of open spaces* becomes the real extension of the house for the its appropriation and diversified use by individuals (Fig. 9).

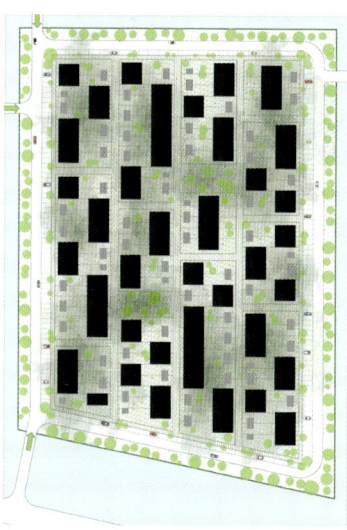

MVRDV, Hageneiland
planimetry with the collective network
of open spaces
Graphic reworking of Paola Branciaroli

NOTES

1. The domestic space is influenced by the culture of belonging, thus the architecture of these spaces takes into account the distances between social and personal space, both referring to the outside part of buildings and the location of activities and objects within the houses (Edward T. Hall).

9

Two projects

Ivan Di Naccio & Marco Di Felice

Kazuyo Seijma & Ass, Sejio Town Houses,
El Croquis n.139/2008
Photo by Hisao Suzuki

Seijo Townhouse – Seijo, Tokyo
Kazuyo Sejima and Ryue Nishizawa (Sanaa)

Seijo is a urban district with a residential character stretching out of sight to the south-west of *Tokyo*. Thickly spread on the territory according to the logic of a computer matrix in which pixels are confusedly turned on and off, its low-rise houses represent the frame of *Sejima* "*Townhouses*", namely a small dense and articulated urban area with a complex sense of spatiality and a strong identity.

Townhouses fit into the neighborhood elaborating the settling principles favouring a new space which is in a dynamic equilibrium between repeatability and uniqueness. The pixels, units of measurement and identity cells of the computer matrix, assume in their architecture translation, the shape of a square-based space module. Meticulously assembled according to an unstable but well-designed order, this module gives life to a fractal geometrical figure whose sense of unity and formative logics are always comprehensible both on a urban scale and on an architectonic one. It features a double and ambivalent dimension which characterizes the project since the beginning and where it is possible to recognize some important theoretical and professional contaminations manifesting the architect willingness to confront him/herself with the urban environment and with the domestic one. As a matter of fact, in the way the project was presented, by means of a white model alluding to its infinite extension on an undifferentiated and almost desert area, it is possible to recognize the theoretical speculations of *Superstudio* (just think about the "*Histograms*", namely regular geometrical shapes covered with white-squared laminates to eliminate shapes favouring an abstract space, or about the "*Supersurface*", a smooth and grilled continuous surface indefinitely extended and freely inhabited) and those of *Archizoom* (think of "*No Stop City*", an anthropic extense of flows and relationships translated from an architectonic point of view into a system of nodes and free connections).

By considering how the complexity and the spatial articulation concentrate in a single housing unit, besides the recent professional experiences of *SANAA* (the design studio by Sejima and Ryue Nishizawa), it is possible to identify the architectural research developed in the last years by *Rem Koolhaas*. His studies focus on the functional congestion and the urban complexity translated and gathered into the single building (just think of the praise to the horizontal skyscraper conceived as an architectural frontier of contemporary living, as theorized in "*Delirious New York*"). In order to get a convincing synthesis of these theoretical and professional experiences, Sejima implements simple and elementary architectural operations defining the overall image of the intervention when applied on the spatial module. Being multiplied into an infinite number of combinations, the modules are in turn matched, aligned, overlapped, inserted, translated...

The *resulting space* is a continuous unfolding of solids and voids alternating and interpenetrating. In this way the interspaces acquire a visual dignity independent from the net volumes delineating the borders. Urban intimate sceneries, private and collective spaces which multiply the opportunities to meet and socialise, reproduce some of the Japanese themes in terms of contemporary living. The house traditionally intended as detached dwelling with garden occupies the first position.

The conjunction of various social factors (population growth, changing of family structures) and environmental factors (rapid urbanization, saturation of metropolitan areas) has pushed private people to invest in collective housing implying a progressive and speculative decline of the living space in the house (165 square meters was the average at the beginning of the century, against the current 85 square meters). Nevertheless, all these elements have not erased the Japanese's conception of house producing, in fact, a deep gap between development and tradition. Acting as a meeting point among different needs, "*Townhouses*" adopt a hybrid typology. For this reason they are considered collective residences even if composed by autonomous units with garden. From an organizational standpoint, in fact, "*Townhouses*" rework some logics peculiar to the Japanese's culture. The houses are small domestic worlds surrounded by sculptural gardens in which interior and exterior spaces seem to be intimately connected, and it is possible to look outside without being noticed. A careful study of openings avoids windows to look onto each other. Thus, housing units and individual houses are equalized even as far as privacy is concerned.

Inside the houses, as for the traditional ones, the rooms are open and free of corridors. There are also some devices reflecting the traditional gestures of the Japanese domestic life: the entrance features an area where people take off their shoes. To guarantee a continuity with the outside space, this area is paved with polished concrete slabs, while the other rooms are paved with wood. Outside, the brick covering performs two different functions, as the whole intervention does:

- urban, to harmonise the whole intervention with the surrounding landscape, characterised by numerous houses with stone or brick cladding;
- architectural, where the brick itself is the dimensional module of volumes as well as the infinitesimal pixel used to measure the whole project.

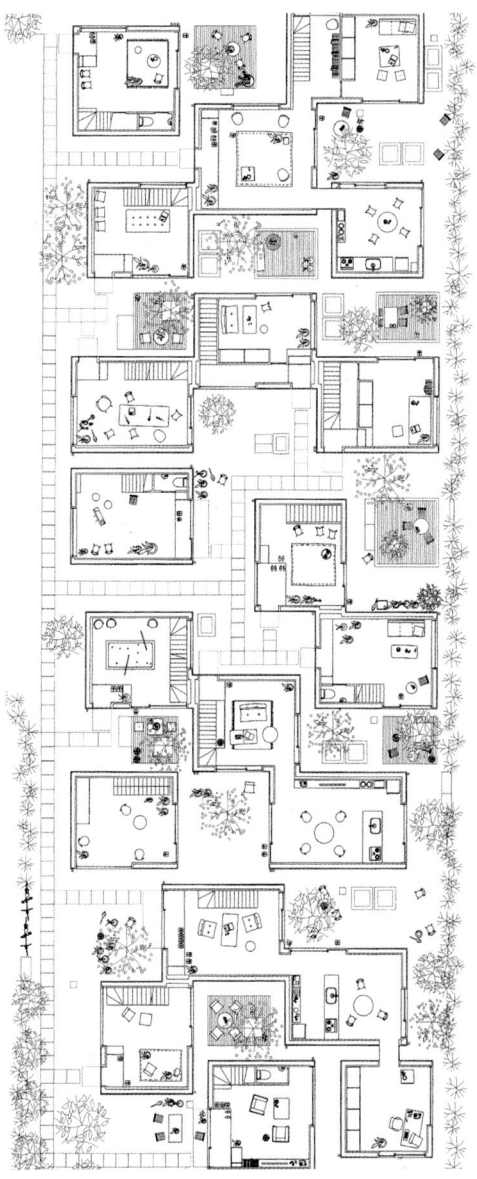

Kazuyo Seijma & Ass., Seijo Town Houses - ground level
El Croquis n.139/2008 SANAA Kazujo Seijma Ryue Nishizawa 2004-08

Along with the versatility of a configuration open to the many possible variations dictated by the multiple needs and different lifestyles of the inhabitants, both in the short and in the long period, it is for this intimate belonging to the social and urban ecosystem that Sejima hopes to extend the project at a local level. If Seijo can be defined as a *Hypercity* (term used by *André Corboz* to define the contemporary city by analogy with hypertext: *"a text is a combination of consecutive paragraphs, printed on paper, usually read from the beginning to the end; a hypertext is a collection of textual data digitalized by means of an electronic medium, and it can be read in different ways"..."a text has a linear structure, hierarchical from the beginning... the hypertext, on the contrary, does not have a univocal and imperative structure"*), then "*Townhouses*", with their fractal grouping logics, become the designed representation, the definitive overtaking of the hypertext on the text.

Finally, a warning: despite the undoubted appeal of these very intimate and articulated spaces, rich in architectural and urban qualities, it is worth noting the distance between this design solution and the set of laws regulating the building industry within the Italian territory. Basements lit by small internal courtyards, walls of buildings grazing each other, windows facing narrow alleys, blind bathrooms: rightly or wrongly, Sejima's "*Townhouses*" would not be feasible within the Italian country.

Ben Van Berkel (UNStudio) –
Water Villa's – Almere – Holland

Almere-Buiten district is, in chronological order, the latest expansion of Almere to the east and marks a sharp boundary between urban and rural area. In that area the city loses its ring development around *Weerwater* and the district merges with the linear, geometrical and fractal scheme of the cultivated fields. Like a composition by *Paul Klee*, they draw the landscape according to an organizational logic in a dynamic equilibrium between order and disorder, form and formlessness, organic and inorganic.

The district was founded thanks to the *Vinex* project (in occasion of the 2001 Building Exhibition), namely a *government development programme including the construction of 750.000 houses within the Dutch territory in the 1995/2005 decade. These buildings had to be organised in experimental neighbourhoods with a planned housing density where the proximity to urban centres and places of work, the connection to the large infrastructure networks and the typological varieties of the residences were granted*. The *masterplan* was given to the architect and urban planner *Teun Koolhaas* who put into the anonymous orthogonal grid of this urban offshoot a diagonal axis with a strong visual and identity impact, a navigable artificial canal bisecting the entire district. From here the residential fabric develops onto the land on its right side and onto an artificial stretch of water with a comb system on its left side.

The designers in charge of the individual plots were asked to develop the following architectonic theme: "*Gewild Wonen*" or "*live according to desire*". It is a clear reference to a structural and programmatic versatility of houses in order to meet the individual and changing needs of future customers. Among all, *Ben Van Berkel (UN Studio)* proposal seems to be the paradigmatic solution for the selected theme. The project consists mainly in the construction of 20 single-family houses orderly located along the left bank of the canal and of 28 row houses positioned on the first two peninsular blocks within the artificial stretch of water. Because of their close relationship with water, they are called "*Water Villa's*" *(WV)*. To meet the request for versatility of the public notice, the WVs highlight a clearly industrial logic (in which there are references to *Functionalism* and *Constructivism*) as to favour an in progress *modus costruendi*. In fact, the final configuration is the result of a spatial module repeated and assembled in predefined ways and, according to the needs, subsequent over time. *WV single-family houses* are made up of two rectangular parallelepipeds of 6x10 meters in plan and 3 meters high and a square one of 6x6 meters in plan and 3 meters high, located on the ground, first and second floors, respectively. By being superimposed they are also rotated and shifted on top of each other. They represent the house standardized original core and in the area shared by the three levels there are the lift system, the bathrooms and the kitchen. The residents can manage all the remaining free and flexible space according to their needs and lifestyles. They can even decide to expand the living surface through rectangular prefabricated modules of 2,5x6 meters in plant and 3 meters high to add to the original core, following the urban planner's project, obtaining a configuration that deeply enhances the dynamic, multi-directional and anti-gravity virtues of the whole.

The *WV single-family houses* have a 150 square meter area in the standard configuration which can extend up to 180 square meters. Outside, a careful use of the coating materials distinguishes the slate original core from the wooden extensions. The openings are brought together into large glass surfaces framed into the walls and positioned so that, in all configurations, they never face, ensuring the right level of privacy to the houses. *The row WVs* are split into groups of two to six units and they face each other along the peninsulas that connect them to

UN Studio van Berkel, Water villa's - houses
Photo by Christian Richters

Water villa's - townhouses - Casabella n.713/2003
Photo by Christian Richters

the mainland. The individual housing units have the same spatial organization of single-family houses: once superimposed, the three modules of the original core are shifted on top of each other (the row configuration does not allow the rotation). The modules alternate their shifts among the single units, so that they are volumetrically distinguishable from each other. As for the single-family *WVs*, also in this case there are modules that, once added to the original core, increase the living surface and strongly dynamize the modules movement. Altogether, the result is a fractal image of the longitudinal sides similar to a huge "filing cabinet" in which the individual residential boxes" are pushed back and forth according to a logic which, far from being accidental, corresponds to the subjective needs of the user.

Division and dynamic movement of volumes represent the *trait d'union* of the intervention, but also the key to understand a language whose roots are based on the Dutch architectural history. The colour contrast of the coating materials dramatizing the plasticity of the movement, the anti-cubic setting and the flexibility of the composition can be understood as the contemporary application of the neoplastic principles, conceived and described in "*Naar een beeldende architectur*" by *Theo Van Doesburg* in 1925. The relationship between *WVs* and the surrounding environment can be seen in the same way. Indeed, it can be synthesized according to different orders of magnitude: physical and metaphysical, material and immaterial, direct and indirect. It is physical, material and direct in trying to interpenetrate with it by projecting the volumes to defy the laws of gravity; in framing and bringing inside the living spaces large rifts of landscape; in filling in with the liquid element reflecting on the surfaces of cantilevered volumes dematerialising the masses. It is metaphysical, immaterial and indirect in conceptually creating, in its intrinsic architectural logics, the balance among those pairs of opposites that unite the design of the landscape to a composition by *Paul Klee*.

Published by
LISt Lab Laboratorio
Internazionale Editoriale
ITALY Piazza Lodron, 9
38100 Trento
tel. +39 0461 1636240
fax. +39 0461 1632045
SPAIN C/ Ferlandina, 53
08001 Barcelona
tel. +34 934422365
mail: info@listlab.eu
website: www.listlab.eu
www.momboo.net

Authors
Rosa Branciaroli, Ilvi Capanna

Editorial Coordination
Pino Scaglione

Editorial assistant
Gioia Marana

Translations
Irene Acler

Art Direction
Massimiliano Scaglione

Graphic Design
Marc Sánchez

Printed by
Printer Trento

Scientific Board of the List Edition:
Eve Blau (Harvard GSD), Maurizio Carta (Università di Palermo), Alberto Clementi (Università di Chieti), Alberto Cecchetto (Università di Venezia), Stefano De Martino (Università di Innsbruck), Corrado Diamantini (Università di Trento), Antonio De Rossi (Università di Torino), Franco Farinelli (Università di Bologna), Carlo Gasparrini (Università di Napoli), Manuel Gausa (Università di Barcellona/Genova), Giovanni Maciocco (Università di Sassari/Alghero), Josè Luis Esteban Penelas (Università di Madrid), Mosè Ricci (Università di Genova), Roger Riewe (Università di Graz), Pino Scaglione (Università di Trento).

Un ringraziamento speciale a Ettore Spalletti e Patrizia Leonelli, Luca Vitone, Walker Art Center e in particolare Karen, Gysin e Pamela Caserta, MVRDV architects (Rotterdam - NL), OeverZaaijer architects (Amsterdam - NL), Segison & Bates architects (London - UK).

All right reserved
© of the edition | dell'edizione, LISt Lab
© of the texts, their authors | dei testi, gli autori
© of the images, their authors | delle immagini, gli autori: pp. cover - 2 Ettore Spalletti

ISBN 9788895623498

Printed in september 2011

Promozione e Distribuzione Internazionale
ActarD/Birkhauser
BARCELONA Roca i Batlle, 2
08023, España
BASEL Viaduktstrasse 42
4051, Switzerland
NEW YORK 151 Grand Street 5th Fl.
NY 10013, Usa
office@actarbirkhauser.com
www.actarbirkhauser.com

List Lab is an editorial workshop, set in Barcelona, works on the contemporary issues. List not only publishes, but also researches, proposes, endeawour, promotes, produces, creates networks.